JAWS
WITHOUT TEETH

Quick answers to atheist questions
designed to shred the Christian faith

JAWS
WITHOUT TEETH

Quick answers to atheist questions
designed to shred the Christian faith

RAY COMFORT

BRIDGE
LOGOS

Alachua, Florida 32615

Bridge-Logos

Alachua, FL 32615 USA

Jaws Without Teeth

by Ray Comfort

Printed in the United States of America.

Library of Congress Catalog Card Number:
  2013946970

International Standard Book Number:
  978-1-61036-116-3

Unless otherwise noted, all Scripture quotations are
from the New King James Version of the Holy Bible.

CH 08-07-13

DEDICATION

To Sherry Pierce—a tireless and faithful soldier of
Jesus Christ.

CONTENTS

FOREWORD

THERE are two keys to reaching atheists. The first is to have a love that is coupled with patience. Many of these people are so blinded by their own undetectable pride that they don't even recognize the love that we have for them. They shoot their rescuers. They are like drunken know-it-all teenagers, with car keys in hand, bent on destruction. Our heart should therefore break for them. While others may write them off as "swine" and withhold pearls of truth, we will plead with them. They are above all men to be pitied, because an atheist doesn't die in the confidence of faith. The best he can have is the weakness of hope. He dies hoping that God and His promise of wrath don't exist.

Love them, buy gifts for them, take them to lunch, treat them with kindness and respect because they are human beings. It is easier to shake our heads with thoughts of saying, "I told you so" on Judgment Day, but the consequences are too great for any of that sort of consolation.

The second key is to make sure that we don't spend too much time addressing their "carnal" mind with apologetics, because that is where they harbor their hostility towards God's moral requirements (see Romans 8:7). Give them answers, but always keep in mind that the Bible tells us that they are "enemies of God *in their minds*" (see Colossians 1:21). So we must make sure we do what Jesus did and address the ally of their conscience, using the moral Law (the Ten Commandments). A. W. Pink said, "Just as the world was not ready for the New Testament before it received the Old, just as the Jews were not prepared for the ministry of Christ until John the Baptist had gone before Him with his clamant call to repentance, so the unsaved are in no condition today for the Gospel till the Law be applied to their hearts, for 'by the Law is the knowledge of sin.'" (Rom. 3:20) It is a waste of time to sow seed on ground which has never been ploughed or spaded! To present the vicarious sacrifice of Christ to those whose dominant passion is to take their fill of sin, is to give that which is holy unto the dogs. What the unconverted need to hear about is the character of Him with whom they have to do, His claims upon them, His righteous demands, and the infinite enormity of disregarding Him and going their own way. You can see the effectiveness of the use of the moral Law on www.GeniusTheMovie.com, and on www.180Movie.com. Please take the time to watch these clips, and *please* take the time to listen to "Hell's Best Kept Secret" and "True and False Conversion." These two free teachings will help immensely in your effectiveness to reach the lost. You will find them on the Home Page of www.Livingwaters.com

For more comprehensive (in depth) answers to difficult questions, see *The Evidence Bible*, and *The Defender's Guide to Life's Tough Questions*.

"The heart of the wise teaches his mouth, and adds learning to his lips" (Proverbs 16:23).

Atheist: "One who believes that there is no deity."[1]

Evolution: "Given enough time and enough accumulated changes, natural selection can create entirely new species. It can turn dinosaurs into birds, apes into humans and amphibious mammals into whales."[2]

---

1. Definition according to Encyclopedia Britannica's Merriam-Webster's Dictionary: http://www.merriam-webster.com/dictionary/atheist

2. Live Science, "What is Darwin's Theory of Evolution?" Ker Than, TechNewsDaily Senior Editor, December 7, 2012, http://www.livescience.com/474-controversy-evolution-works.html

QUICK ANSWERS TO COMPLEX QUESTIONS

ASKED BY ATHEISTS

1. **"If your God was so great, I would see no reason why He would need to force people to submit to Him in worship."**
   a. We are free to be unthankful for our eyesight, hearing, food, sunlight, and all the pleasures He has lavished onto us. But if we die in our sins, we will get justice. That's why we need a Savior. When He opens our eyes through the new birth, worship comes as easily as songs do to an early morning songbird.

2. **"Did the American Native Indians credit their conscience to your Jesus?"**
   a. Not until they heard the gospel. They knew that there was a Great Spirit who made all things, and the Gospel put a Name to Him.

3. **"If I were God, I'd hate to have you people speaking on my behalf."**
   a. We do our best, but we are fully aware that "God has chosen the foolishness of preaching to save those who believe" (see 1 Corinthians 1:21). He chose the weak vessels of human beings to take the

message of everlasting life to weak and dying human beings.

4. **"What happens to those who never get a chance to hear the Gospel and die before they do get a chance?"**

   a. No one will go to Hell because they haven't heard of Jesus. They will be condemned for murder, rape, adultery, fornication, lying, stealing, etc. Put your concern for others to hear the gospel aside for the moment. If you die right now you will end up in Hell. Get right with God and become a missionary, if you really care about the lost.

5. **"Everyone is born atheist."**

   a. No one is "born" an atheist. If you really believe that, then trees and puppies are atheists. They begin life with no belief in God.

6. **"Do you wear cotton poly blend?"**

   a. Polyester blends cause static and sweat. I far prefer the coolness of pure cotton. It makes sense that in the hot Middle East climate, God told the Hebrew people not to mix materials.

7. **"Why doesn't God heal amputees?"**

   a. Why doesn't He grow hair on bald heads, make short people tall, replace missing teeth, cut my grass, and find my lost car keys? Why does He put up with

people who ask mindless questions?
We don't know. One thing we do know
is that He is holy and perfect, and we
have to face Him on Judgment Day.

8. **"Why did God create us sick then command us to be well?"**

   a. When God made Adam, everything was
   "very good" (see Genesis 1:31). There
   was no disease, pain, suffering and death.
   These miseries came when Adam sinned.
   God cursed the ground and gave Adam
   and his offspring the death sentence.
   The Bible says that we "die in Adam,"
   but we can be "made alive in Christ"
   (see 1 Corinthians 15:22). You are free
   to ignore God's command to repent and
   trust in the Savior, but if you do, instead
   of receiving mercy, you will get justice.

9. **"Have you given everything away yet?"**

   a. Nowhere in Scripture are Christians told
   to give everything away. Rather, we are
   told the opposite—to take care of our
   loved ones by providing for them
   (see 1 Timothy 5:8).

10. **"So why, oh, why did He create us, then destroy us, then repopulate us through incest if He had foreknowledge of exactly what we were about to do?"**

    a. He didn't "destroy us." We are still here
    despite the flood of Noah—because God

in His kindness saved eight people, and He didn't repopulate us through incest because "incest" wasn't a sin or a crime in those days.

11. **"About 90% of prison inmates in America are religious. Roughly 75% are Christian. Roughly the same amount of serial killers are Christian."**

    a. Christians obey the law and love their enemies—they don't murder them. Religious hypocrites (pretenders) violate the law and kill people. They will be sorted out and punished on Judgment Day.

12. **"My life is great. I'm good without God."**

    a. All of us think we have our own definition of "good." But "good" in God's Book means moral perfection, in thought, word, and in deed. That will be the standard of judgment on Judgment Day. If you think you have a great life, you will want to keep it.

13. **"Are you a meat eater?"**

    a. When Jesus told the Parable of the Prodigal Son, He didn't say to "kill the fatted cabbage." He said to kill the fatted calf. They had a barbeque. The Bible teaches that Christians are free to eat or not eat meat (see Romans 14).

14. **"Galileo was censured by the church, and**

he's far from the only example. When the church would claim dominion over that which rightfully belongs to science, then atheists have every right to be angry at it for preventing human advancement. Would we have ever landed on the moon if the church had kept convincing everyone the Earth was flat?"

a. Galileo wasn't an atheist. When the Roman Catholic church confined him to house arrest he protested, "I do not feel obliged to believe that the same God who has endowed us with sense, reason, and intellect has intended us to forgo their use." Also, almost everyone (including scientists) believed that the earth was flat (except theist Christopher Columbus and some others). And don't forget that the men who landed on the moon read Genesis chapter one from space, and just before the landing they took communion and thanked God for sending a Savior.

15. "The creator of the Internet, a homosexual, and Bill Gates, who gave away billions to help humanity, and the creator of FaceBook, and other atheists... are all going to Hell?"

a. Being rich or inventing something doesn't mean that you get an automatic

11

pass if you violate criminal law. Anyone who has violated God's Law (the Ten Commandments) will end up in Hell, irrespective of how rich they are or what they've invented. Bill Gates is not an atheist.[1]

16. **"We don't know how we came here, but let's study and try to find out and not give a simple answer like 'God.'"**

  a. Atheists don't like God being the answer to that question. That's like saying, "We don't know what two plus two adds up to, so let's not give a simple answer like 'four.'"

17. **"I am single; how is having lustful thoughts adultery?"**

  a. When someone physically commits adultery they violate the Seventh of the Ten Commandments (even if they are single), and in God's eyes if we as much as lust, that Commandment is broken. We may have a definition of adultery,

---

1. *The Telegraph* reported, "It does force us to sit down with the Pakistan government to renew their commitments, see what they're going to do in security and make changes to protect the women who are doing God's work and getting out to these children and delivering the vaccine." Source: "Bill Gates interview: I have no use for money. This is God's work." *The Telegraph*, 18 Jan 2013, http://www.telegraph.co.uk/technology/bill-gates/9812672/Bill-Gates-interview-I-have-no-use-for-money.-This-is-Gods-work.html

but God's definition is much higher.

18. **"How did Judas die—did he hang himself, or did he fall headlong and his bowels gushed out?"**

    a. He hung himself, and unsurprisingly his still-hanging and decomposed body fell to the earth and split open. There is no contradiction.

19. **"Are you scared to publicly say that Islam is of Satan, Muhammad is a false prophet, and Allah is not God—Islam is a false religion and it is your personal aim to wipe out Islam."'**

    a. It's not the aim of Christians to wipe out Islam. We want every Moslem to make it to Heaven, and we therefore lovingly share the gospel with them.

20. **"If properly read, the Bible is the greatest resource for atheism man ever wrote."**

    a. Please encourage people to read it.

21. **"Do gays go to Hell?"**

    a. "Do not be deceived. Neither fornicators, nor idolaters, nor adulterers, nor homosexuals, nor sodomites, nor thieves, nor covetous, nor drunkards, nor revilers, nor extortioners will inherit the kingdom of God" (1 Corinthians 6:9–10). This is God's standard. If you don't like it feel free to take it up with Him.

22. **"Did Judas or did the Pharisees buy a**

field with the 30 pieces of silver?"

a. The Pharisees used his money that he had thrown down to buy a field in his name. There is no contradiction.

23. **"Evolution is a proven fact."**

a. The burden of proof lies with the believer in evolution, but there is no proof because nothing can be observed. How can that which supposedly happened over millions of years, be observed? It is all founded on faith in men's ideas, old bones, and in fallible dating methods.

24. **"What proof is there Jesus ever existed?"**

a. Those who ask this question apparently don't know what year it is.[2]

25. **"If you believe that the world is going to come to an end, does it not drain one's motivation to improve life on earth while we're here?"**

a. We desperately want to improve life on earth by stopping the mass-killing of the unborn through abortion, the rape of women, pornography, greed, lying, child abuse, murder, theft, adultery, wife-beating, hatred, wars, etc. The heart of the human problem is the sinful heart of the human being, and the only power

2. We take our date "since Christ".

that can change that is the gospel.

26. **"Didn't men write the Bible?"**

   a. Men wrote the Bible, but they wrote it in the same way a pen is instrumental in writing a letter. Men were God's instruments to pen His letter to humanity. His signature is on the letter through the amazing prophecies of the Bible. Only He knows the future.

27. **"Suffering proves there's no God."**

   a. It proves the opposite. The truth of the Bible is substantiated by what we see around us, because it tells us in Genesis that we have suffering, disease, pain and death because we live in a "fallen" creation.

28. **"The Bible is full of mistakes."**

   a. It has *seeming* mistakes, which, when investigated with a humble heart, prove to be *our* mistakes, not God's. The death of Judas, the day Adam died, the "two" creations, the last words of Jesus, etc., all have simple explanations.

29. **"Why doesn't God show Himself?"**

   a. No man can look upon God and live. The Bible says that He shines above the brightness of the sun. If we stood in His presence, His justice would spill over and execute us for our crimes against His Law. He, however, has made Himself known through His creation. The order of nature shows us His handiwork and leaves us without excuse (see Romans 1:20–24).

30. **"There is no Hell."**

   a. If a judge shut his eyes to Mafia murders, he is a corrupt judge, and should be prosecuted himself. If God is good He must see that perfect justice is done. The Bible warns that that will happen on Judgment Day. God will punish all murderers and rapists, but He is so good, and so just, He will also punish thieves, liars, fornicators, adulterers, and even those who have lusted (see Matthew 5:27–28) and hated (see 1 John 3:15). Hell is His terrible prison, and those who go there won't be eligible for parole.

31. **"Do you believe in talking snakes?"**

   a. Parrots talk. Dogs tell humans when there's danger. They also "talk" with other dogs. Dolphins communicate with each other. So do whales. Elephant's converse with each other, and a cat will tell you when he's hungry. Believers in evolution mock the thought of a snake that can communicate, but they believe that they themselves are talking primates.[3]

32. "Creationism is anti-science."

    a. Creationism can be observed. Genesis says every animal has male and female and brings forth after its own kind (see Genesis 1). Faith isn't necessary when it comes to what the Bible says about these things, because this is observable in the existing creation and in the fossil record.

33. "Blasphemy is a victimless crime."

    a. Atheists should think more deeply about their self-incriminating words. They themselves call blasphemy "a crime."

34. "Can God make an object He cannot lift?"

    a. With God, nothing is impossible.

35. "Which 'God' are you talking about: Thor, Zeus, etc.?"

    a. There are millions of gods (Hindus have 450 million). There is only One Creator. He's the One you must face on Judgment Day. Worshipping any other god is a violation of the first of the Ten Commandments.

---

3. The Smithsonian Institute: "How Do We Know Humans Are Primates?"—"Besides similar anatomy and behavior, there is DNA evidence. It confirms that humans are primates and that modern humans and chimpanzees diverged from a common ancestor between 8 and 6 million years ago." http://humanorigins.si.edu/resources/how-do-we-know-humans-are-primates-0

36. **"What's funny to me is that the religious people get on a social networking site developed by an atheist (Mark Zuckerberg and FaceBook), using operating systems created by an atheist (Apple's Steve Jobs, Microsoft's Bill Gates)...and talk about how atheists are damned, doomed to hell and the world is better off without them."**

    a. Steve Jobs was not an atheist. Just after his tragic death in October, 2011, National Public Radio said, "Jobs told Isaacson [his biographer] that he was '50/50' on the existence of God, and that he wasn't sure whether there was an afterlife."[4] Nor is Bill Gates.

37. **"Why did God order the killing of an entire people group? That's genocide."**

    a. God didn't just kill a group of people. He killed the entire human race, except for eight people, in the Noahic flood. You should thank Him for saving them, because without them, you wouldn't be here. You will also die because God has ordered your death sentence. However, He will grant everlasting life to those

---

4. "New Bio Quotes Jobs On God, Gates And Great Design," October 25,th, 2011, http://www.npr.org/2011/10/25/141656955/new-bio-quotes-jobs-on-god-gates-and-great-design

who repent and trust in Jesus.

38. "If I'm made in God's image, why do I have a vestigial tail?"

a. It's not a "tailbone." It's the coccyx vertebrae, and it anchors 12 important muscles: "The tailbone derived its name because some people believe it is a 'leftover' part from human evolution, though the notion that the tailbone serves no purpose is wrong. The coccyx is an extremely important source of attachment for tendons, ligaments, and muscles, though it is structured quite differently than other parts of the spine."[5]

39. "I thought God was supposed to be our friend, not our enemy."

a. The Bible says that we are enemies of God in our mind, in a state of continual hostility towards the God of the Bible (see Romans 8:7). However, He will become your friend, if you surrender to Him (see John 15:14).

40. "How can you justify God killing everyone in a flood?"

a. God doesn't have to justify Himself to anybody, because He is God. Everyone will die, because the Judge of the

---

5. Laser Spine Institute: "Tailbone." http://www.laserspin-einstitute.com/back_problems/spinal_anatomy/tailbone/

Universe has proclaimed our death sentence. We are the ones who need justification, not God, and we can be justified through repentance and faith in Jesus.

41. **"Why does the Old Testament show a God of wrath and the New Testament a God of mercy?"**

   a. There is no difference between the two. God is just as loving in the Old Testament and just as wrath filled in the New Testament. He never changes.

42. **"Who made God?"**

   a. God created the dimension of time, but He isn't subject to it. He dwells in eternity where there is no time, and it is eternity into which you will pass, when you pass on.

43. **"Why does God want to torture people in Hell?"**

   a. Hell is God's prison, where there will be no parole. It is where those who have done evil (violated His moral Law) will receive perfect justice. Call that torture if you will—all the more reason not to end up there.

44. **"The Bible is not backed up by archeology; it's disproven in many cases by archeology."**

   a. The exact opposite is true. You need

only do an Internet search using the
words "archeology and the Bible."[6]

45. "There's no scientific evidence of a god!"

    a. Those who make such claims need
absolute knowledge. Somewhere in the
universe there may be knowledge they
haven't yet come across, which could
be ample evidence. They are therefore
forced to say that "as far as I know"
there is no evidence. The word "science"
simply means knowledge, and there
is enough knowledge in the order of
Nature that proves that God exists.

46. "Christians are obsessed with death."

    a. Only yours… We have eternal life.

**47. "If God does exist, how do you explain
incurable genetic diseases, cancer, and
needless suffering?"**

    a. If you reject the Genesis curse, nothing
makes sense. The Bible says we live in
a "fallen" creation—filled with disease,
suffering and death.

**48. "I have not been a perfect person
at times, but I have tried to make
things right."**

    a. If you are guilty in a criminal court of
a serious crime, you can't make things
right yourself. If you are guilty, there

---

6. http://christiananswers.net/archaeology/

must be punishment. Our crimes against God are so serious they demand the death penalty.

49. **"Jesus appealed to God on the cross when He himself is God, supposedly."**

    a. When God, the omnipresent Upholder of the Universe, became a Man, He didn't cease to be the omnipresent Upholder of the Universe. He was limited to time and space, and called God His Father.

50. **"The belief that we are sheep in need of a shepherd is disgusting and revolting to me. To consider my intellect equal to that of a sheep is an insult to my dignity."**

    a. Only believers are likened to sheep (teachable). Unbelievers are likened to goats (stubborn).

51. **"A morally good God would judge people based on who they define themselves as through actions, not thoughts or belief."**

    a. Our thoughts and beliefs govern our actions, and God considers lust to be adultery and hatred to be murder. That's His standard and there is no changing that. Anything else is a form of idolatry.

52. **"I was a Christian for 25 years."**

    a. During your time as a Christian, did you know the Lord? If you say that you did know Him, you are admitting that

God is real. If you say that you *thought* you did, then you didn't, and you were never a Christian. You faked it all that time. But you are not alone. Many, if not most atheists, have had false conversions and that's why they are so adamantly anti-Christian. They heard a false gospel that said that Jesus gives joy and peace and fixes problems, and when what they think is Christianity didn't deliver the promised goods, they became disillusioned and often bitter.

53. "There is no proof that God exists."

   a. Atheists believe the scientific impossibility that nothing created everything. That is the automatic default when someone believes that there was no initial Cause. They have only one alternative, and that is to redefine the word "nothing" to be *something*. Some do that, confirming the Bible's wisdom in reminding us that "The fool has said in his heart, there is no God."

54. "None of you know what God would say to anybody."

   a. We can know God's will. He left us His last will and testament. I would advise you to begin reading His will by checking out the New Testament, because He has left an inheritance.

55. **"Hitler was also a self-proclaimed Christian."**

    a. He was a Roman Catholic who hated biblical Christianity. He called it a "disease."

56. **"If you believe the earth is 6000 years old then you deny science."**

    a. If you believe the earth is millions or billions of years old, you "believe" science. You don't "know" the age of the earth. You "trust" what you've been told by fallible men and fallible dating processes. Your convictions rest entirely on faith.

57. **"I swapped my Bible for a copy of Thomas Paine's, 'The Age of Reason.'"**

    a. For no reason, eternal pleasure was swapped for nothing but Paine.

58. **"I lack belief in gods." (Part One)**

    a. Atheist, PZ Myers said, "Boy, I really do hate these guys. You've got a discussion going, talking about why you're an atheist, or what atheism should mean to the community, or some such topic that is dealing with our ideas and society, and some smug $@!#* comes along and announces that 'Atheism means you lack a belief in gods. Nothing more. Quit trying to add meaning to the term.' As if atheism can only be some

24

platonic ideal floating in virtual space with no connections to anything else; as if atheists are people who have attained a Zen-like ideal, their minds a void, containing nothing but atheism, which itself is nothing."[7]

59. "I lack belief in gods." (Part Two)

   a. Atheist, PZ Myers said, "I have heard this so often, the hair-splitting grammatical distinctions some atheists think so seriously important in defining themselves. All you're doing is defining yourselves as #$%!@ retentive freaks, people! Get over it. Either way, you're an atheist—and that goes for the over— philosophized fussbudgets who insist that they're agnostics, not atheists, because they aren't 100% positive there aren't any gods, only 99 44/100ths positive."[8]

60. "There are 3,000 gods that you don't believe in. I just don't believe in one more."

   a. There are not 3,000 gods. There are millions (Hinduism has 450,000,000). Making an image of god (either with your hands or in your mind) is called "idolatry" and is a violation of

7. http://scienceblogs.com/pharyngula/2011/02/01/why-are-you-an-atheist/

8. Ibid

the First and the Second of the Ten Commandments. However, there is only one Creator, and He is the One you have to face on Judgment Day whether you believe in Him or not.

61. **"Glaciers created the Great Lakes, and tectonic plates created mountains."**

    a. The word "created" is a figure of speech. Lakes are simply "melted" glaciers. Nothing was created. The rain doesn't create puddles on the ground. The puddles are merely rain on the ground.

62. **"What about the appendix? It's a left-over from evolution."**

    a. The appendix is said to be vestigial. But it's not. Duke University said: "Appendix Isn't Useless at All: It's a Safe House for Bacteria, By Duke Medicine News and Communications. Long denigrated as vestigial or useless, the appendix now appears to have a reason to be—as a 'safe house' for the beneficial bacteria living in the human gut."[9]

63. **"Why was it okay for Lot to allow his daughters to get raped? Is that what God believes to be moral?"**

    a. The Bible is full of people who did stupid things. They are in the Bible as

---

9. http://www.dukehealth.org/health_library/news/10151

examples of what not to do.

64. **"What did the 3,000 species of termites eat on Noah's boat for 10 months?"**

    a. There's only one "kind" of termite. The first couple probably just dined on one piece of wood during the flood.

65. **"Every evangelist says give to Jesus, but they give me *their* address."**

    a. The Bible prophesied of them: "But there were also false prophets among the people, even as there will be false teachers among you, who will secretly bring in destructive heresies, even denying the Lord who bought them, and bring on themselves swift destruction. And many will follow their destructive ways, because of whom the way of truth will be blasphemed. By covetousness they will exploit you with deceptive words; for a long time their judgment has not been idle, and their destruction does not slumber" (2 Peter 2:1–3).

66. **"If God designed our bodies, He didn't do a very good job."**

    a. Maybe yours isn't very good. Remember that we live in a fallen creation filled with disease, pain, suffering and death.

67. **"After Jesus died, the Apostles created Christian communism—'If you read the Sermon on the Mount of Jesus Christ,**

and the Moral Code of the Builder of Communism – they are identical.'"[10]

a. Jesus said to love your enemies and to do good to those who despitefully use you—communism slaughtered 110 million people.[11] They couldn't be more opposed one to another.

68. **"I have found that I do not have to believe in God to be good."**

a. Everyone is good, by their own low moral standard. When God says "good," He means moral perfection, in thought, word, and in deed.

69. **"Have you guys read the part about not judging lest ye be judged?"**

a. This verse of the Bible is directed at Christians, in the context of not judging other Christians. It goes hand in hand with Romans 14, which is about Christians judging each other as to what they should eat, drink, etc. Later on in the same portion of Scripture (Sermon on the Mount) Jesus said that when we judge, we should use "righteous judgment."[12]

---

10. http://rt.com/politics/
   christ-first-communist-communist-party-leader/

11. HOW MANY DID COMMUNIST REGIMES MUR-DER? By R.J. Rummel, "In sum the communist probably have murdered something like 110,000,000." http://www.hawaii.edu/powerkills/COM.ART.HTM

12. John 7:24

70. **"So, because I accept evolution I'm going to hell?"**

    a. You can believe in the Easter Bunny, if you wish. People will go to Hell for murder, rape, lying, stealing, adultery, fornication, lust, pride, etc. Each of us desperately need the Savior.

71. **"Macro [evolution—changes in kinds] is just the sum of micro [non-evolution—variations within kinds]."**

    a. This is not true. Micro evolution (changes *within* a "kind"—differing species of dogs, etc.) is everywhere, and it has nothing to do with Darwinian evolution (one "kind" changing *into* another "kind"). It's an excuse to hide bogus science behind the skirts of what we see in nature.

72. **"The universe may have always existed. It does not need a Creator."**

    a. That is scientifically impossible, because of the 2nd law of thermodynamics. Everything is corrupting. If the universe was eternal it would have turned to dust billions upon billions of years ago. Only God is eternal because He is not physical. He is Spirit.[13]

73. **"If your God is omnipotent, why do**

---

13. John 4:24

thousands of children starve to death every single day?"

a. An estimated 40 thousand children die of starvation each day. Many die because of political regimes that refuse to allow aid into their countries. Others die because God withholds the rain from their land. Less would die if rich nations were more generous with their abundance of food. Back in 2010, the U.S. spent about $18.7 billion dollars on space exploration.

74. **"Considering having someone killed because another person didn't do something right, seems a bit ridiculous."**

a. What Adam did may seem ridiculous, but God holds you personally responsible for your own actions. If you fall off a cliff, gravity will kill you. If you place your finger in a live light socket, electricity will kill you. These are the natural consequences that God has created for violators. You are violating God's moral Law at the moment, but you feel secure because you don't see the full consequences. But they will eventually come.

75. **"The Bible says 'God repented.' Doesn't that show He is capable of sin?"**

a. In the context, it simply means a

change of mind. This is different than repentance as regards to sin.

76. "How can a perfect God be wrath filled?"

a. A good judge should be furious if an unrepentant mass murderer has raped and viciously taken the lives of a number of innocent teenage girls. If he wasn't angered, he wouldn't be a good judge. God is good (morally perfect) and He is therefore greatly angered by evil.

77. "You can't compare God with a human judge."

a. That's right. God is infinitely more just and holy, and He warns that He will by no means leave the guilty unpunished.[14]

78. "God is unfair in that Hitler and a sweet old lady (who never trusted in Jesus) will both go to Hell."

a. The Bible speaks of degrees of punishment. Everyone will get exactly what they deserve; and this includes those young people who have grown old. Time doesn't forgive sin.

79. "My God would never create Hell."

a. Idolatry is the sin of making up our own god. The God of creation is the One we must face, and He warns that ultimate justice will ultimately be done, no matter

---

14. Exodus 34:7

31

what we do or don't believe.

80. **"If God is loving, why would He send people to a place of torment?"**

   a. A judge may be a loving man, but if he is good he must see that justice is done. However, because of God's love, His justice was satisfied at the cross so that people could escape Hell.

81. **"If God doesn't hear some prayers, how can He be omniscient?"**

   a. Our sins make a separation between us and God. He resists the proud and gives grace to the humble. Psalm 66:18 says that if I have sin in my heart "the Lord will not hear me." In other words the ungodly don't have His ready ear unless they approach Him in humility.

82. **"I don't believe God is knowable."**

   a. What we "believe" is irrelevant. If we believed that the sun was made of ice, it wouldn't change reality. Truth is what matters, and the truth is that human beings can come to know God.

83. **"If God created the sun on the fourth day, how do you know four days passed?"**

   a. A "day" is 24 hours. It isn't dependent on the sun. Alaska doesn't see the sun for months and yet they still have "days."

84. **"God in the Old Testament murdered thousands of people for insignificant**

crimes. Someone today who does that is labeled a maniacal psychopath and is locked away."

a. How do you feel about abortion?

85. **"How could God see what He was doing before He created the sun?"**

    a. The Scriptures say, "Indeed, the darkness shall not hide from You, but the night shines as the day; the darkness and the light are both alike to You" (Psalm 139:12).

86. **"Faith is for children; faith that a fat man will visit them once a year and leave presents."**

    a. However, that is faith in a non-existent entity. Those who trust in the Living God will never be disappointed.

87. **"Faith is relative to where you live on the planet."**

    a. True. There are millions of Hindus in India and Christians in the United States. However, salvation is a work of God, and God is not restricted to any location. If people in the heart of darkest Africa seek God, He will see to it that they hear the gospel.[15]

88. **"An atheist doesn't believe that nothing created everything."**

---

15. "And you will seek Me and find Me, when you search for Me with all your heart" (Jeremiah 29:13).

a. Atheists say that they have "no belief in a god." If I have a car and have no belief in a maker of the car, it, by default, means that I think that the car made itself—or that no one made it.

89. **"There is proof of evolution. Have you noticed how children are taller these days? Welcome to observed evolution, change over time."**

   a. That isn't Darwinian evolution. That's adaptation within the human kind. It has nothing to do with evolution. There has been no change of "kinds."

90. **"How come Christians don't stone adulterers anymore?"**

   a. Why would Christians follow 3,000 year-old Hebrew criminal law? If someone violates American law in America, we prosecute them under American law.

91. **"If nothing can come from nothing, your god had to come from somewhere as well."**

   a. Not if He was Spirit, eternal, and created the dimension of time. God qualifies for all three.

92. **"Psalm 137:9 tells you that God will bless you if you bash a child's head in against a rock."**

   a. It says no such thing. The Psalmist

was lamenting the terrible cruelty of
the Babylonians, praying that God
would treat them as they had treated
their captives.

93. **"That's why the world loves Christians.
Invade a country with Bibles and fear
of Hell."**

   a. There is one thing you don't seem to
   consider—the reality of Hell. When you
   find that it does exist, you will suddenly
   see that we loved you and pleaded with
   you, and all you did was mock us. And
   all we can do is keep pleading. We love
   you and deeply care about where you
   spend eternity.

94. **"You people are being good for a reward.
I'm being good because I care about my
fellow human beings."**

   a. Being a Christian has nothing to do
   with being good (that's the deception
   of "religious" people). We can't earn
   eternal life by being good, because we
   are criminals in God's eyes. Anything we
   offer Him in the area of "good" works
   is in truth an attempt to bribe Him to
   dismiss our case.

95. **"I'll wait until I am old, then I'll get
right with God."**

   a. You may not get the chance. Jesus told
   of a man who boasted that he had so

many material goods that he would
have to build bigger barns. God called
the man a fool and death took him
that night.

96. **"The Bible is the oral history of bronze
age sheep herders, written down.
They really didn't know much about
why things happened. ...Just sit down
and read it, start to finish. You will
understand better."**

   a. The Bible will make sense when you
   come to know the Author. It is filled
   with history of an ancient people, but it
   also tells you how to get everlasting life.
   You seemed to have missed that part.

97. **"Many of the predictions of Nostradamus
came true. Will you start equating him
with divinity?"**

   a. Nostradamus was a lapsed Jewish
   Catholic that read his Bible in secret and
   stole its prophecies, without giving God
   attribution. Anyone who is ignorant of
   Bible prophecy will be impressed with
   the prophecies of Nostradamus. The
   rest of his ramblings are so nebulous
   anyone can look down through history
   and hang anything on them. That's why
   Nostradamus is a billion dollar industry.

98. **"What about the law to stone the woman
taken into adultery...is Jesus saying that**

God is wrong to command that she be stoned."

a. This woman, who was taken in the very act of adultery, is like each of us. We have been caught in the act of breaking the Ten Commandments, and the moral Law calls for our death. However, God can completely forgive us because Jesus took the wrath of the Law upon Himself. That means we, like the woman, can have our case dismissed. There is no compromise because the Law is satisfied by the suffering of the cross. So take a lesson from the Scriptures. Thank God for His mercy, then like the woman, trust in Jesus, go your way and sin no more.

99. **"Is infinite punishment the proper response to a finite crime?"**

a. We look at eternality in reference to the dimension of time. However, when we die we will pass on into eternity, where there is no time. One act of disobedience in Eden resulted in death and in all the pain and suffering we have seen throughout history. This is a reflection of the perfect holiness of God. Each of us has sinned against Him a multitude of times, the seriousness of which will be seen on Judgment Day.

100. **"If I'm wrong, I'll go to Hell and party like a madman in Hell for all eternity. I can't lose!!"**

   a. There will be no pleasure in Hell; just thirst, loneliness, fear and pain, forever.

101. **"I can sin and cheat and lie and kill as much as I like, but just before I die, I become reborn. My murdered victim is in Hell, but me, just because I said, I want Jesus in my heart, just before they injected me goes to Heaven?"**

   a. Don't worry; no innocent person will go to Hell. Instead, be thankful that God is rich in mercy towards guilty sinners like you and me.

102. **"Only a sick person would create us as sinners and then threaten us to get better on pain of death."**

   a. Tragic though it is that we have inherited a sinful Adamic nature, we are morally responsible for our sins. "Adam made me do it" is no defense in criminal court, and it won't be a defense on the Day of Judgment.

103. **"Sin was constructed by Christians in order to dominate and control the weak."**

   a. It may be true that religion has been used to control the masses; however, the concept of sin wasn't invented by

Christians. "Sin" is just another word for evil, and evil—murder, rape, theft, etc., happens every day.

104. **"God loves you so much He invented Hell just in case you don't love him back."**

    a. It is a crime against God not to love Him with all of our heart, mind, soul, and strength—for who He is and for the gift of life. But ingratitude is only one of the multitude of sins the best of us has.

105. **"How do you explain the millions of children that He lets perish from starvation?"**

    a. If you are an atheist, He doesn't let any children starve to death, because He doesn't exist. If you believe in evolution it's simply a matter of survival of the fittest.

106. **"I do not believe in evolution. I do not choose what I believe. I am compelled to believe what I believe by the presentation of evidence which leads only to one logical conclusion. ...That is why we believe it."**

    a. Look at your words: "I do not believe... what I believe...what I believe...that's why we believe." Evolution is completely faith-based. It's a belief. Nothing is observable without having to exercise a blind faith.

107. "The Bible is a story book, just like a book of Fairy Tales."

a. The Bible may look like a book of fairytales—if you deny the supernatural. A right understanding of the power of God opens the door to the normally impossible.

108. "What if I ask God to reveal Himself and it turns out to be Allah?"

a. Then you are in bigger trouble, because Islam also believes in Hell, but they have no Savior.

109. "The Bible is rife with historical inaccuracies."

a. To provide evidence for such a claim you will need to have faith in history books that were written by fallible men. The Bible was written by men who were inspired by an infallible God, and so it is 100% historically accurate. Not believing the Scriptures doesn't change that fact.

110. "If God created cancer, He is bad."

a. If God created cancer, then He is real and you have to face Him on Judgment Day, guilty of a multitude of crimes against His Law. You will be on trial on that Day, not God.

111. "How do I know God exists?"

a. There are at least two evidences. One

is creation. It is scientifically impossible
for Nature to create itself. The second
is your conscience. God has given you
moral knowledge of right and wrong.
It is shaped by society, but given to you
by your Creator, so you are without
excuse for your crimes against His Law.

112. "It sounds like the God of the Ten Commandments is jealous and angry."

a. His "jealousy" is not a sinful human
jealousy. His attributes and ways are
always in perfect righteousness.

113. "The Bible is simply outdated."

a. While it is filled with ancient laws that
God gave to the Hebrew nation, it tells
tomorrow's news before it happens.
See Matthew 24, Luke 21, 1 Timothy 4,
2 Timothy 3 for some examples.

114. "I don't hate God. I just don't believe He exists."

a. There is no greater contempt that you
can have for another person than to, in
their presence, deny that they exist.

115. "Christians are mean-spirited and I reckon about as far away from what Jesus seemed to be about as you could get."

a. Jesus spoke of sin, God's perfect
righteousness, and of the existence of
Hell. He said the world would hate Him

because He accused them of sin, and
that they would hate Christians because
they belonged to Him. You are guilty of
making up your own Jesus (something
the Bible calls "idolatry").

116. **"What about goosebumps? What is
their function?"**

a. Perhaps you could believe that
Goosebumps are evolutionary evidence
we evolved from geese. In truth,
they close up the skin so that it
retains warmth.

117. **"Jews laugh at Christianity."**

a. The disciples were Jewish. The first
13,000 converts were Jewish, Christianity
was birthed in the land of the Jews, the
New Testament was written by Jews,
and we accept the Jewish Old Testament
as the Word of God. Any Jew who
believes their God-breathed Scriptures
will embrace Jesus of Nazareth as their
promised Messiah.

118. **Atheist: "Ray's site has sure revealed why
the U.S. is behind in education. Religion
keeps you dumb, that's for sure."**

a. Christian: "They don't teach
'religion' in schools anymore....They
teach evolution."

119. **"I allowed God to come into my life
for 20 straight years—20 years was long**

enough, time is up. I'm not a bad person nor am I a sinner."

a. A false convert makes a profession of faith with no knowledge of sin, and because they didn't repent they didn't come to know the Lord. Most fall away from their church in time. Others stay, and will be sorted out on Judgment Day.

120. **"You have to love everyone to get into Heaven, but then you have to hate everyone to get into Heaven. There are flaws....flaws, everywhere!!"**

a. No one will get to Heaven by loving anyone or everyone. Eternal life is a free gift of God. Nothing we do can earn it. There are no flaws. The Bible often uses "hyperbole," by contrasting love and hate, for emphasis.

121. **"Do you believe your way is the only way into Heaven?"**

a. It's not my way. Jesus is the One who said that no one can get to God but through Him. While we may be confused as to which (of all the different denominations) is right, God knows those that love Him. Those that love him obey Him by trusting in the Savior He provided, and they are the ones that will be in Heaven.

122. **"Which is the right God?"**

a. There is only one Creator—that's the One who gave Moses the Ten Commandments, the One who provided the only Savior—the One who can save you from a very real Hell. Jesus said, "If any man will do his will, he shall know of the doctrine, whether it be of God, or whether I speak of myself" (John 7:17). Do the will of God—repent and trust in Jesus, and you will know the truth.[16]

123. **"If there is a Judgment Day, my good deeds will eliminate the bad deeds."**

a. That doesn't even work in a court of law, and it won't work on Judgment Day. If a criminal has committed a very serious crime, his good deeds will not wash away his crimes, and our sins against God are so serious they warrant the death sentence.

124. **"Over 30,000 denominations of the Christian church and not one can agree with the other!"**

a. Most of those denominations agree on the basic tenants of the Christian faith. Only on non-essential doctrines there is disagreement. However, it's human nature to disagree about almost everything. I'm sure you would agree with that.

---

16. See John 8:31–21.

125. "Hell doesn't exist. Sorry for bursting your bubble."

a. When did you get knowledge of the afterlife? Do you have connections with the other side? The truth is that you don't know what happens after someone dies, and you could know, if you believed the Bible. It is appointed to man once to die, and after this the Judgment.

126. "Why pray? Who are you to ask God to alter His plans?"

a. It is a mystery that God would condescend to use the prayers of humble men and women to shape the destiny of humanity, but that doesn't change the fact that He does. We speak to Him through prayer, and He speaks to us through His Word, the Bible.

127. "Pascal's wager is a flawed argument, thoroughly debunked."

a. It is impossible to debunk Pascal's famous wager. He simply said that the Bible says that if you come to Christ you gain everlasting life. If you don't, you end up in Hell. By becoming a Christian you can't lose. If you are right you gain everlasting life, and if you are wrong and there's no afterlife, you won't even know it. So it's a win/win situation for the Christian and lose/lose situation for the ungodly.

128. **"We've just discovered that the universe is actually 50 million years older than we thought. Oh. And it's also possible that we'll be able to explain what there was BEFORE the Big Bang. Here's a clue, it wasn't a dude with flowing robes, a fluffy white beard and a questionable set of morals."**

   a. I don't know why you are saying "We've" just discovered. What you mean is "They've" just discovered, and you have faith in whatever "They" say. You are an unquestioning and faithful believer. And you are right. It wasn't a dude with a fluffy white beard.

129. **"People have been waiting for Judgment Day since the introduction of Christianity."**

   a. The Bible predicts that skeptics would say this, and they do so because they don't know that God created time and dwells outside of its dimension. The Bibles says a day to the Lord is a thousand years to us. He is patiently waiting, not willing that any perish, but that all come to repentance.[17]

---

17. 2 Peter 3:8,9

130. "I've never sinned."

　　a. One of you is lying—it's either you or God, and the Scriptures say that it is impossible for God to lie.[18] Romans 3:23 says "all" have sinned.

131. "I was raised in an Atheist family. I was unaware of Christianity until I went to school. Doesn't that show that God is not always there for people?"

　　a. God is "always there," but He's not the world's Divine Butler. He doesn't come running when we click our fingers. The Bible says that if you seek Him with all of your heart, you will find Him.[19] Why should you seek Him?—Because He is the source of everlasting life, and yours is running out by the minute.

132. "While you religious nuts are using your hands to pray for starving children, I use mine to actually feed them at the food pantry."

　　a. I think you may be misjudging a lot of people with that remark. Christian organizations like World Vision (and many others) feed and clothe millions around the world. There are hundreds, if not thousands of Christian rescue

---

18. See Hebrews 6:18

19. Jeremiah 29:13

missions that every day feed, clothe, and house the poor.

133. "You can't prove God is real."

    a. Creation is proof that there is a Creator. It is impossible for Nature to have made itself. However, God will prove Himself to you in the same way you can prove electricity is real. If you don't believe in it, put a fork into a live light socket. The Bible says that you will receive "power" when the Holy Spirit comes upon you.[20] God will give you the shock of your life, if you obey Him. Read John 14:21.

134. "You are just talking to some imaginary Friend."

    a. That is true for a proud atheist who tries prayer. The Bible says that God will not hear your prayers because your sins separate you from Him.[21] The proud do talk to the ceiling, because God is not some imaginary Friend, but a very real enemy.[22] That's the teaching of Scripture.

135. "Hitler was undoubtedly a Christian."

    a. Hitler said, "Our epoch will certainly see

---

20. See Acts 1:8

21. See Isaiah 59:1

22. See Colossians 1:21

the end of the disease of Christianity,"[23] "Christianity is the worst of the regressions that mankind can ever have undergone,"[24] "The heaviest blow that ever struck humanity was the coming of Christianity."[25] Adolf Hitler was a lapsed Roman Catholic, who hated Christianity. He knew that there was a difference, but for some reason atheists say they don't, revealing their willful ignorance of the Scriptures.

136. "Is the Bible literally true?"

a. All of Scripture is inspired by God.[26] Some parts are literal, some figurative. When Jesus said that He is the door He didn't mean a literal door with hinges, but that He is the way of entry into Heaven.[27]

137. "Science is presented with new evidence that changes. You will continue to justify the same old story despite the evidence."

a. Truth doesn't change. Error does. What evolutionary believers believe now, will change in the future and then it will

---

23. Hitler's Table Talk, pg 343–344

24. Hitler's Table Talk, pg 322

25. Hitler's Table Talk, pg 7

26. See 2 Timothy 3:16

27. See John 10:7–9

change again. They can never know
anything for certain.

**138. "The Bible explains nothing. It still
leaves you with the infinite creation
loop regress."**

a. The Bible explains everything—from
our origins, our purpose, our destiny,
to why there is death and suffering, and
how to find everlasting life. However,
these truths are hidden from the
proud heart.[28]

**139. "I guarantee all you so called God—
believers go to a doctor if you get cancer,
heart problems, kidney disease, etc. If
you truly believed you would pray and
expect Him to heal you."**

a. Of course we pray, and we go to doctors.
The two are not mutually exclusive. The
Bible says that the prayer of faith will
save the sick[29] and that having a merry
heart (being happy) does good "like a
medicine."[30] Medicine is good.

140. "We are primates."

a. You may think and act like an animal,
but that doesn't change the fact that God
holds you morally accountable and you

---

28. See Luke 10:21

29. See James 5:15

30. See Proverbs 17:22

have to face Him on Judgment Day, whether you believe in Him or not.

141. **"There is a strong correlation between religious belief and a lower intelligence level though."**

   a. That's a matter of perspective. We are not the ones who believe that we are talking primates[31] and are cousins of bananas[32] (as atheist, Richard Dawkins, believes).

142. **"Save your prayers, I'm quite comfortable with myself in my own faith and comfortable enough to know if God exists, the God who created this beautiful star, he won't be the God of the Bible or any other man made religion on this planet. No loving God would brutally slaughter every man, woman and child of this planet in the Great Flood, pregnant women drowning at the bottom of the ocean, children screaming for help as the crushing waves devour them, just because a few people ticked him off. He wouldn't**

---

31. "We admit that we are like apes, but we seldom realize that we are apes." Richard Dawkins, *A Devil's Chaplain: Reflections on Hope, Lies, Science, and Love*

32. "It is a plain truth that we are cousins of chimpanzees, somewhat more distant cousins of monkeys, more distant cousins still of aardvarks and manatees, yet more distant cousins of bananas and turnips … continue the list as long as desired." Richard Dawkins, *The Greatest Show on Earth: The Evidence for Evolution*

be the tyrannical dictator of the Old Testament. Of that I am sure."

a. Your "image" of a loving god is even more tyrannical, because if he created us, he coldly stands back and lets millions starve, allows rape and murder—and lets Hitler slaughter six million Jews. He gives no explanation, refuses to bring justice to the wicked, and leaves us all hopeless in the face of death. However, the God of the Bible will bring final justice to all evil, and in His great kindness offers everlasting life to guilty sinners.

143. **"He who can look into the eyes of a crack addicted baby, a newborn with horrible birth defects, a newborn riddled with cancer, or a newborn who will probably die before it recognizes what life is, and say 'It's God's plan' or 'God works in mysterious ways,' or just think that it's perfectly fine, is a truly disgusting person, and doesn't deserve to be a part of society."**

a. All human suffering and death are the result of the Genesis Fall. What we see on earth isn't God's perfect will. It is His *permissive* will. However, the day will come when God's will, will be done on earth, as it is in Heaven. Don't miss out on being part of the eternal kingdom, because it certainly is coming as Jesus said it would. You and I don't deserve to be part of that kingdom, but God says we may.

144. "What is 'sin'"?

a. It is the breaking of God's moral Law— the Ten Commandments.[33]

145. "Why did God let the talking serpent into the garden of Eden knowing what he would do?"

a. No one can answer that but God. Make peace with Him and if you ask in humility, He may reveal it to you. In the meanwhile, don't end up in Hell being punished for your many sins, just because this bothers you.

146. "Why did God not smite Lucifer for his betrayal when He so easily smote so many others for far lesser crimes?"

a. What you consider lesser crimes were apparently not.

147. "A God of unconditional love would NEVER put conditions on that love. Hell is a condition."

a. The "god" you don't believe in doesn't exist. It's called "idolatry" when you make up false gods (a violation of the First Commandment). Nowhere does the

---

33. See 1 John 3:4

Bible say that God has "unconditional" love. He is a God of justice and holiness, and you have to face Him on Judgment Day whether or not you believe in Him. Hell is not a "condition." It's a very real place of punishment.

148. **"Why does God command that infants should be dashed upon the rocks"?**[34]

    a. He doesn't. The Babylonians, who conquered and enslaved Israel, were very cruel, and apparently they killed infants in such a way. The Psalmist is understandably seeking vengeance, and doesn't even mention God when he says, "O daughter of Babylon, who are to be destroyed, happy the one who repays you as you have served us! Happy the one who takes and dashes your little ones against the rock!"

149. **"Bottom line—when you declare you have faith in something—you are literally proclaiming you have no evidence, but choose to believe anyways."**

    a. I have faith in my wife, and it's based on the evidence of knowing her for years. She is impeccably trustworthy. It's even more so when it comes to trusting God. Bottom line—we have thousands of

---

34. See Psalm 137:9

years of His faithfulness, laid out for us in the Scriptures.

150. **"If someone suddenly, and without a shadow of a doubt, disproved your God today, would you go out and start raping and pillaging?"**

   a. I certainly hope not. However, we have rape and pillaging, murder, and a whole lot of evil happening in society because many people either believe God doesn't exist or they think that He won't punish them.

151. **"Spiritualty and religion was first expressed in India."**

   a. Spirituality was first expressed when God created Adam and Eve, in the beginning. They talked with the Spirit of God face to face.[35]

152. **"Impaled on a cross as an expression of love? How is that not twisted and masochistic?"**

   a. Only those who understand that they have violated God's Law can appreciate the fine being paid on their behalf.

153. **"He who looks into the eyes of a newborn baby and says that child is evil and born of sin and will go to Hell if not baptized is seriously mentally ill."**

---

35. See Genesis 1–3.

    a. You are confused. The Bible doesn't
    say anywhere (or even hint) that if a
    newborn baby isn't baptized, it goes
    to Hell.

**154. "I don't hate God. I just don't believe
He exists."**

    a. Such is the way of many cultures that
    if a son or daughter marries out of the
    faith or does something of which they
    strongly disagree, in the parent's minds,
    they no longer exist. There is no greater
    contempt for a person than to so hate
    them they don't exist in your mind.

155. "Christianity is a guilt trip!"

    a. Which of the Ten Commandments
    makes you feel guilty, and why?

**156. "Someone you love more than life itself
dies and goes to Hell, and you die shortly
after and go to Heaven. Is it truly Heaven
without that person beside you?"**

    a. Heaven is a location, not a mere state of
    mind. God is the Creator of all things.
    With Him, nothing is impossible,
    and He says that He will give pleasure
    forevermore. Not believing that doesn't
    change reality.

**157. "Why should I be punished for
something some woman ages ago did?"**

    a. Although you have inherited a sinful
    nature from Adam and Eve, you are

morally responsible to God for your actions. That defense wouldn't work in a court of law, and neither will it work on Judgment Day.

158. **"Atheists do not have faith that a God does not exist, we are just asking for the evidence that a God exists."**

   a. Creation is evidence for the existence of God. It is scientifically impossible for nature to make itself. See Romans 1:20–24. You are without excuse now and will be on Judgment Day, if you are without a Savior.

159. **"Even if the Universe did have a supernatural or natural creator, it is not proof that such a creator is anything like the one portrayed in the Bible."**

   a. That's true. But your problem is that the God of the Bible is the only one who provided a Savior. Without Jesus Christ you will die in your sins and end up in a terrible place called Hell. No religion or effort on your part can save you from Eternal Justice.

160. **"I am full of life and happiness. My family brings me joy, among other things. I love living in the here and now, and being accountable to my fellow humans."**

   a. Everything you love is temporal. It will

one day be ripped from your hands by death. That could be today—and that's not some sort of scare tactic; it is reality.

161. "Suppose the Muslim hell is the real one. Then YOU lose."

    a. Muslims aren't fools. They know the Creator exists because of the order of Nature and the existence of the human conscience. They also know that Hell exists, but they have no Savior to avoid it. God provided a Savior for all of humanity. He said that "whoever" trusts in Him will be saved. This is truly good news for the whole world.

162. "Atheists are free-thinkers."

    a. Anyone who believes that nothing created everything isn't a free-thinker. He is free *from* thinking. The Bible calls him a "fool" (see Psalm 14:1).

163. "If God wants us all to follow and worship Him, why didn't He create us as such?"

    a. When He created Adam and Eve, they were without sin. But when they disobeyed God, sin entered their hearts and then passed it on to their offspring. When you are born again[36] God makes

---

36. See John 3:1–5

you a new creation.[37]

164. "Believers are supposed to live humble lives, not lives filled with smart phones, laptops, big houses, nice clothes and fancy cars."

a. A Christian can be humble and be rich. There is nothing wrong with money. Rather the Bible warns that the *love of money* (not money) is the root of all kinds of evil.[38] In Scripture, those who are rich are told to use their wealth for good.[39]

165. "He who sees the eyes of a child beaten and molested while his God watched is a seriously sick person for believing in a God."

a. It is thoughtless to jump to the conclusion that nothing created everything, simply because God doesn't immediately punish evil. If He intervened and had Judgment Day today, where would you stand under the light of moral perfection? God is holding back from punishing child molesters, rapists, adulterers, fornicators, homosexuals, those who lust, hate, lie, steal and covet,

---

37. See 2 Corinthians 5:17

38. See 1 Timothy 6:10

39. See 1 Timothy 6:17

because He is rich in mercy and willing to forgive all who repent and trust in Jesus.[40]

166. **"We'll leave you alone as soon as you realize not everyone shares the same beliefs and keep your beliefs in your homes and churches where they belong... none of us have the right to impose our beliefs on each other. The human race will be in a much better place when religious people learn this."**

   a. We won't be keeping the gospel to ourselves, our homes, or our churches. We are going to use every medium possible to shout the message of everlasting life from the housetops. We're coming at you to tell you that eternal life is the free gift of God—and that no one needs to end up in Hell—including you. We deeply care about you and where you spend eternity, even if you don't.

167. **"If Christianity worked, you would not be seeing the emergence of the age of reason... but you are witnessing its birth."**

   a. Atheism—the age of reason? It is leading us back into the dark ages—of talking primates, we are made of stardust, we are cousins of bananas, believing in walking

---

40. See 2 Peter 3:9

whales, spinning through space on a
planet made by nothing for no reason
at all.

168. **"God murdered millions."**

   a. God never "murders" anyone. He is
   a righteous Judge, and you have been
   given the death sentence (along with
   every other human being). However, He's
   rich in mercy and offers you a reprieve.
   Take it or leave it—life or death, Heaven
   or Hell.

169. **"I do not fear death, in view of the
   fact that I had been dead for billions
   and billions of years before I was born,
   and had not suffered the slightest
   inconvenience from it. None of us are
   eternal. Make most of the here and now,
   or throw away the joys this world offers
   in this fleeting time we have in existence
   for the false promise of eternal bliss."**

   a. Why did you say "billions and billions"?
   Why not "trillions and trillions"? I will
   tell you why. Because what you meant
   was that you were "eternally" dead,
   but you dare not use the word
   "eternal" because it has connotations
   of you-know-Who.

170. **"The only thing that disappoints me
   about the lack of afterlife is that you
   loons will never even have that moment**

where you realize you were wrong all along. I almost wish you would, and I'd love to be there to see it!"

a. We don't think the same of you. When you find out that God is morally perfect and that Hell is real, there won't be anything in us that says "We told you so." We're horrified at the thought of you facing absolute justice and being justly damned forever.

171. **"Have you ever heard of someone who grew a limb? No... why does God always cure the easy stuff that the body can do on its own?"**

a. Have you ever heard of God growing hair on bald heads, making short people tall, replacing knocked out teeth, or making fat people skinny? I'm sure you haven't. How could you then leap over logic and reason, and say that He doesn't exist because you haven't seen Him do such things?

172. **"The biggest loser is he who lives in fear of an imaginary punishment and in hope of an imaginary reward, instead of appreciating that this is the only life we have."**

a. You are convinced that this one life is the only life we have. You no doubt have based this on the knowledge that when someone dies it's all over because there is no life in the body. This is because the life has left the body. There is no brain activity because it is the life that gives the brain its activity.

173. "Why do Christian women still have period pains and childbirth pains if Jesus died for their sins?"

a. Christians will be under the Genesis curse right up until the time when God removes it from creation. When Jesus suffered and died for our sins, He purchased our redemption. When God's Kingdom comes to this earth and God's will is done on this earth as it is in Heaven, we will take custody of the purchased possession.

174. "Lack of faith is insulting to God—sounds extremely petty."

a. I don't believe for one minute any word you say. You are not a trustworthy person. I lack faith in you because you lack the virtue of faithfulness.[41]

175. "If there was an omnipotent Supreme Being, why would He use such a fallible device of communication—a book written by men, selected by men? Why not just communicate directly?"

---

41. See 1 John 1:10 and 1 John 5:10

a. God did communicate directly with human beings. When He gave the Ten Commandments, the nation of Israel was so fearful that they thought they would die. He has chosen to give us His written Word telling us how to find everlasting life, and we are to simply do what it says.

176. **"A whale was found with atavistic hind limbs of over 4 feet long. This makes perfect sense according to an evolutionary framework. Please explain how it makes any sense according to creationism."**

   a. Do an Internet search for "photos of extra limbs" and you will find lambs with eight legs, people with four legs, three arms, etc. They have nothing to do with evolution and neither does a whale that has extra limbs.

177. **"The only thing you can say about all atheists is that they all lack belief in gods."**

   a. There are many atheists around the world who don't embrace your carefully worded modern definition. They simply say "I believe that there is no God." Your cut-and-paste movement only started a few years ago. But you are still connected to the old "I believe" atheists. If I have a car and say "I lack belief in makers," it means I believe that cars have no makers—and my car therefore had no maker. It means that I believe that nothing made it. So, carefully worded though your modern definition may be, it still leaves you believing the scientifically impossible—that nothing made everything.

178. **"Why is it that God destroyed Sodom and Gomorrah but had no problem with Adam, Eve and their two sons basically procreating the world?"**

a. Adam and Eve obviously had more children. Two men cannot procreate.

179. **"Why is it that God gives AIDS to kids in Africa?"**

a. As an atheist, God didn't give them AIDS because He doesn't exist. Always keep that in mind when you blame Him for things when you don't believe He exists. If He did commit the crimes you accuse Him of, then He exists and you have to face him on Judgment Day.

180. **"Jesus asked Himself if this cup could pass him by. He didn't listen to Himself."**

a. When the Creator and Upholder of the Universe made a human body and filled that body as a hand fills a glove (Jesus was "the express image of the

65

invisible God"[42]) He didn't cease to be the omnipotent Creator and Upholder of all things. Jesus was fully Man and fully God, but in the incarnation He was limited to time, space, hunger, thirst, all so that He could suffer the pain of death[43], to save us from Eternal Justice.

181. "Please explain why I should get down on my knees and start pleasing an immoral, judgmental, childish, inferior, insecure, genocidal maniac God!"

a. You are the one who is immoral, judgmental, childish, inferior, insecure, self-righteous, blasphemous and godless—with the ultimate delusion of grandeur in thinking that you can stand in moral judgment over Almighty God. You need to look closely at your own sins in the light of the Ten Commandments.

182. "God is evil, so I don't really care if I offend Him. He offends me."

a. As an atheist are you saying that He's real? Check out Romans 8:7 for why He is offensive to you.[44] It will show you

---

42. See Hebrews 1:1–3, John 1:1–12.

43. See Hebrews 2:9

44. "Because the carnal mind is enmity against God: for it is not subject to the law of God, neither indeed can be" (Romans 8:7).

your core motive.

183. **"I'd love to see the creationists response when we do finally make some or other form of life. The day is coming.... science, you gotta love it."**

   a. All the combined brains of our most intelligent scientists haven't a clue how to even begin to make one grain of sand from nothing, let alone create the utter complexity of even one cell of organic life. It is comparatively simple to recreate, using God's existing materials, but we can't make the simplest thing from nothing. Such utter human powerlessness reveals the intellectual embarrassment of atheism.

184. **"I'm looking forward to joining Abraham Lincoln, Mark Twain, Charles Darwin, Bill Gates, and Albert Einstein in Hell, while you can be with Adolph Hitler. LOL. If only it was true."**

   a. None of the above were atheists. Not even Hitler. Hitler was a Roman Catholic, who used God for political gain. The rest were theists. Einstein didn't believe in a "personal" God, and hated it when he was called an atheist.

185. **"I can be a good person without God."**

   a. Anyone of us can be good without God. All we need is a very low standard

of goodness. There are 46 dictionary
definitions of "good" from which to
choose. The word "good" in God's
Book, however, means moral perfection,
in thought, word and in deed. That's
the high standard of goodness that we
be will judged by on Judgment Day
(whether you believe in God or not).

186. **"I can kill someone, but just
before I die, I become reborn. But the
person I killed will end up in Hell. How
is that justice?**

   a. God will do that which is right. You
   need not concern yourself with who He
   saves, or who He damns. Just make sure
   you are right with Him yourself.

187. **"I don't know how anyone can tell me
with a straight face that an all-forgiving,
all-loving, compassionate God would
condemn anyone to eternal pain and
agony in the bowels of Hell for eternity
just for the actions of a mere 90 years on
this planet."**

   a. The Bible doesn't say that God is all-
   forgiving and all-loving. You are creating
   an "idol"—making up a false god in
   your mind. God is holy and just as well
   as loving and merciful. His love is seen
   in that He gave you the gift of life. His
   mercy is seen in allowing you to sin

against Him. But if you refuse to repent and end up dying in your sins, He will give you absolute justice, and that's a fearful thing. Damnation means forever being damned from all the pleasures He lavished upon you, for which you were so unthankful.

188. "You can accept both evolution and God. They're not incompatible."

a. God made Adam in His image.[45] Neither God nor Adam was an ape. Jesus said, "In the beginning God made them "male and female." He didn't make them as primordial soup.[46]

189. "My conscience is clear because I follow some practices of Buddhism."

a. A rapist can tell the judge that his conscience is clear because, in his mind, the woman he raped asked for it by her provocative dress. A clear conscience isn't the issue. On Judgment Day forgiveness of sins is the only thing that will matter. It will be the difference between innocent or guilty, life or death, Heaven or Hell. Forgiveness of sins can only come through the cross.

190. "Pray for us and we will think for you!"

---

45. Genesis 1:27

46. http://leiwenwu.tripod.com/primordials.htm

a. That's all we are trying to get you to do. Think. Think about your eternal salvation. Think about the genius of God's creative hand. Think about your sins. Think about the Savior and what He did on the cross.

191. **"Isaiah 7:14: 'Therefore the Lord himself shall give you a sign; Behold, a virgin shall conceive, and bear a son, and shall call his name Immanuel.' Christians say that this verse is a prophecy of Jesus' birth to a virgin. Virgin in this verse is a mistranslation of the Hebrew word *almah*, which actually means 'young woman.'"**

a. You say that miraculous sign was that "a young woman" would give birth. How could that be a "sign" from God? Billions of young women have given birth. The sign was that a *virgin* would conceive. That's a sign.

192. **"I have no faith. Please do not try and bring me down to that level."**

a. So you have no one you trust. I guess you are insecure. You even sound paranoid. Paranoid people refuse to trust people or things. They live in fear. They have no faith in banks, the police, planes or elevators. Paranoid: "Exhibiting or characterized by extreme and irrational fear or distrust of others."

193. **"I went to church four days ago. I liked the preacher because he didn't yell and scream and tell me I was going to hell. He smiled the whole time he talked. Why can't more of them be like that?"**

    a. We won't yell and scream at you, but we will warn you that if you die in your sins, you will end up in Hell. You ending up in Hell doesn't seem to worry your smiley preacher though.

194. **"No one is confident there is no God. There is just no evidence that proves there is a God."**

    a. You should have said that you haven't yet found proof that God exists. Otherwise you are claiming omniscience (having all knowledge) when you say that "no one is confident there is a God," and only God has that.

195. **"Science is about observation and testability. God fails terribly every time it comes to those standards."**

    a. Darwinian evolution is unobservable and untestable. That's why it is so faith-based. We know God exists because of Nature/creation (observation), and He is testable because He reveals Himself to all who obey Him (see John 14:21).

196. **"God loves everyone, but I read in Romans 9, 'Jacob I loved and Esau I hated.'**

What do you make of that?"

a. Most interpret that as "hyperbole" (a justified exaggeration for contrast). However, when God "hates," it is judicial and not sinful.

197. "Does God love all the 20,000,000 people he killed in the Bible?"

a. The Bible says that God takes no pleasure in the death of the wicked. In the end it will be far more than a mere 20 million that God puts to death. All of us will die, because all of us have sinned[47].

198. "Does God hate the wicked? Or does he just hate the wicked things they do?"

a. Scripture makes it clear that God has a judicial hatred for wicked men.[48] This is different than the sinful hatred you and I may have, because God is without sin.

199. "It was Christians that slaughtered millions of Native American Indians."

a. Christians don't slaughter anybody. Sinful man does in the name of God. He always has, and he always will. Saying that Christians killed millions of Indians is about as fair as saying atheists

---

47. See Romans 6:23

48. See Psalm 11:5

killed 110 million through atheistic
Communism. The problem isn't atheism
or religion. It's sinful men.

200. **"According to the book of Deuteronomy,
the cost of keeping an unwed virgin
which I have raped is 50 silver shekels.
Is that correct?"**

   a. If you study the verses, you will see that
   the sex was consensual. We call it
   a shotgun wedding.

201. **"It would seem that the Baptists may
actually lead the Catholics in child
molestation convictions."**

   a. The entire international Church is filled
   with false converts/hypocrites. Let's hope
   the law exposes paedophiles before they
   get to the kids. Otherwise God will sort
   them out on Judgment Day.

202. **"Do you really believe in talking snakes
and talking donkeys?"**

   a. Would you consider yourself to be a
   talking primate?

203. **"You also need to remember that
blasphemy only counts if you believe.
Many non deists do not recognize
blasphemy since they have nothing to
blaspheme against."**

   a. That's like saying, "Judge, you need
   to remember that rape only counts if
   you believe it is rape. I don't recognize

rape." It is amazing that anyone who purports to be intelligent would think that something doesn't exist just because he or she doesn't believe in it. If I don't believe in the sun because it's cloudy, it doesn't disappear just because of my lack of belief.

204. **"Is there any amount of evidence that could be provided to you that would make you not believe in the God of the Bible?"**

    a. Questions like this one show that atheists have no idea that Christians don't merely believe that God exists. They know God.[49] It's like asking a newly married man, "Is there any evidence that I can give that would make you not believe that your wife exists?"

205. **"How did we get our days of the week?"**

    a. They show up automatically just after midnight. Perhaps you need to reword the question.

206. **"Keep up the good work, Ray! I myself can't thank you for being the reason for my de-conversion, but I'm sure there is plenty out there who can."**

    a. My life has been devoted to exposing the hypocrites in the Church, and, with the

---

49. See John 17:3

help of God, seeing them awakened to their delusional state. But there are still plenty of more false converts faking it and deceiving themselves. Let's hope they admit that they don't know the Lord, and repent and trust the Savior, before Judgment Day.

207. **"On TED it talks about the brain of a fly. Go look it up, it's amazing. They compare the fly's brain to a human brain. The fly's brain is way more efficient than ours."**

a. Proof of that is that there are people who think it wasn't the product of Intelligent Design.

208. **"Religion destroys cognitive thinking and replaces it with blind trust in lies intended only to control people. If mankind is to avoid untimely extinction, it has to mature past being willfully ignorant. That, my friends, is a cause worth fighting for on any front you can."**

a. You sound like some doom's day prophet, playing on people's fears. You have a concern that humanity will become extinct? What about evolution? It will fix everything. Relax. It did it without you once, and it can do it without you, once again.

209. **"I would start with *Origin of Species* and**

> read the 1000+ books written on the topic since then. How many books prove God? Oh right, one."

a. You will read another thousand and not find proof for evolution. The whole belief rests on faith. I read every page of *Origin of Species* and it was drier than a ten year-old peanut butter sandwich. The Bible doesn't prove God. It doesn't need to. We know that God exists because of the incredible order of Nature and our God-given conscience. It is simply the Instruction Book for those who know Him.

210. **"God forces victims to marry their rapists."**

a. Not so. The sex in the commonly cited verse, is consensual (Deuteronomy 22:28–29). Nowadays we call it a shotgun wedding. The previous verse will tell you that God gives the death sentence to rapists. That's how much He cares about the victim.

211. **"Why does God tell people to own slaves?"**

a. If a Hebrew was in debt he could work off that debt by being a "bond-servant" or "slave." We put negative connotations on the word "slave" because Americans kidnapped Africans, sold them as bond-servants and treated them with great cruelty. God prescribed the death sentence for kidnapping.

212. **"God told Abraham to sacrifice his son to prove his love."**

   a. God told Abraham to "offer" Isaac, and when he was about to kill him, God stopped him (see Genesis 22). This is a Bible "image"—of God sending His "only begotten Son" to suffer for the sin of the world. Any dirt we try and throw at God will always come back down on us, because He is without sin.

213. **"The First Commandment says, 'You shall have no other gods before Me'— that proves He isn't the only God!"**

   a. There are millions of false gods (Hinduism has hundreds of millions). Man gravitates towards idols (which he makes with his hands or with his mind), because they don't demand moral accountability.

214. **"Which one's a bigger fool Ray? The person who rationalizes and decides to do things for himself like ask questions, critically analyze things, do research and use scientific methods in order to figure out things in life or the person who blindly listens to every word of a 2000 year old shepherd's journal written**

in the bronze age of a superstitious era
by a collaboration of sheep herders that
claims to have all the answers to every
possible question imaginable which in
fact had been interpreted and translated
throughout several generations until it
ended up in the hands of a mad king
who re-wrote it and intentionally left out
information and altered it in a way that
he saw fit?" (quoted verbatim)

a. You have to learn to use the period.
   I needed paramedics by the time
   I finished reading your 114-word
   sentence.

COMFORT QUOTES

ATHEISM:

1. Atheists blame a God they don't believe exists killing everyone in the world-wide flood they don't believe happened.

2. The atheist shuts off His God-given light and then walks in darkness, not knowing his origins, his purpose, or his destiny, thinking that he's intelligent.

3. When Solomon said that there's nothing new under the sun, he may have been talking about the arguments put forward by atheists.

4. We can't buy heaven through religion and neither can we deny heaven through atheism.

5. He is thoughtless indeed who says that no one knows if there's an afterlife, and then says that there's no afterlife.

6. The atheist who thinks that he wins the argument in this life will lose it in the next—and that's the one that matters.

7. Dreams can temporarily convince the dreamer that the insane is reality. Such is the way of atheism.

8. Atheism is oblivious to the obvious, blind to the seeable, and ignorant to the knowable.

9. It is foolish to think that atheists are

intelligent, when the Bible says that they are fools.

10. A thought-provoking question to ask an atheist is whether or not he thinks that his brain was intelligently designed.

11. Every breath drawn by those who hide behind the delusion of atheism is a testimony to the mercy and patience of God.

12. How shallow are those who don't believe in the invisible: air, love, history, television waves, energy, radio waves, and gravity.

13. It is true irony, when an atheist deems himself to be wise.

14. Atheists who are angry that God told Joshua to kill people are angry about something they believe didn't happen.

15. Richard Dawkins is the pied piper of a generation who love his tune of guilt-free sin.

16. There are no atheists in severe turbulence.

17. Atheists, who accuse God of Old Testament atrocities, can't possibly win. If God doesn't exist, there were no atrocities. If He committed the crimes, He exists—and so does the Day of Judgment.

18. Atheists believe that they don't have faith.

19. Atheists scoff at the argument that a building is proof of a builder, saying that a building is inorganic, that it isn't "life." I wonder what they think mountains,

soil, rivers, clouds, sunlight, and oceans are made of.

20. The childishness of name-calling God "sky daddy" and "spaghetti monster" confirms that, with the atheist, we are dealing with fools.

21. All the evidence in the world about God will never convince an atheist who is in love with his sin.

22. "Intelligent atheist" and "evolutionary science" are duel winners of the Mother of all oxymoron's.

23. Talking with an atheist is like trying to reason with someone who denies the existence of the sun.

24. "Goodbye" is one word that atheists should delete from their vocabulary. It's from Old English: "God be with ye."

25. He is a fool who blasphemes the name of the One who is in charge of lightning.

26. A blind man can see more of God when told about a humming bird, than the atheist sees in the whole realm of nature.

27. Atheist groups who hinder people from coming to Christ have strong ties with millstone ministries.

28. Arguments and excuses are thin bushes behind which the atheist thinks he hides from God.

29. The atheist argument isn't about evolution,

science, or the existence of God. It's about love for sin.

30. The atheist who believes that atheism is a no-brainer, is right. It's a denial of reason, logic, intellect, and the inner light that God has given to every man.

31. Atheists who keep asking for evidence of God's existence are like a fish in the Pacific Ocean wanting evidence of water (see Romans 1:18–20).

32. The slowest of theists is infinitely more intelligent that the most intelligent atheist, because an atheist believes that nothing created everything—a scientific impossibility.

33. The atheist who says that there's no evidence that Jesus Christ ever existed, mustn't know what year it is.

34. The Bible's revelation that man is willingly ignorant is never as evident as in the rebellion of atheism.

35. Atheism is the graveyard of false converts, and modern evangelism is burying them there.

36. The silence must be deafening after a sneeze at an atheist gathering.

37. An atheist doesn't see the forest or the trees.

38. Those who know The Lord know their Bible and say no to atheism.

39. He who looks into the eyes of a newborn baby and says that there is no God is more

than senseless, mindless and brainless.

40. That man is willingly ignorant of God
is never as evident as in the rebellion
of atheism.

41. Read God's Word as you would dig for gold
nuggets. Tragically, most atheists don't see
any because they only look for dirt.

42. There is no greater contempt for someone,
than to live your life as though they
don't exist.

43. There's no word more fitting than the
biblical word "lost" to describe a world that
is ignorant of its origins, of its purpose, and
of its eternal destiny.

44. Biblical prophecy stands as a stark warning
to unbelievers that God's fingerprint is all
over the Bible.

45. Trying to remove God from society is
like trying to remove the air from the
earth's atmosphere.

46. The gauntlet for any honest skeptic:
"If anyone wills to do His will, he shall
know concerning the doctrine" (John 7:17).

47. When you say "When you're dead, you're
dead," please realize that you are only dead
to this life, because you have passed on to
the next.

48. High-rollers have nothing on the atheist.
He plays Russian roulette with a fully
loaded gun.

49. List the top ten things you love about your life: color, beauty, food, friendship, laughter, music, peace, joy, pleasure and family. Then kiss them goodbye forever, if you die in your sins.

EVOLUTION

1. Evolution is illegitimate science hiding behind the coattails of legitimate science.
2. The difference between the tooth fairy and Darwinian evolution is that kids are eventually told the truth about the tooth fairy.
3. Close examination of evolution proves it to be nothing but a mirage.
4. If Charles Darwin knew what we know about the complexity of the cell, he would have dropped his fantasy faster than a flea hops onto the back of a mangy dog.
5. Darwinian evolution is unscientific, unobservable, unbelievable, but understandable in a world that hates God.
6. Darwinian evolution is based on blind faith, because nothing is observable. The best they have is bacteria evolving into bacteria and that's not Darwinian evolution.
7. Evolution gives its believers temporary license for guilt-free sexual pleasure—it deals with the problem of moral accountably.
8. Darwin's fantasy was one small step

for a man, but a giant leap backwards
for mankind.

9. Evolution is the modern opiate of
the masses.

10. Never in the history of humanity has there
been a farce as ridiculous as the theory
of evolution.

11. If you want to play the numbers game
with "Thousands of scientists believe in
evolution!" *Billions* believe in creationism.
We win.

12. "Proofs" for evolution are continually
evolving, and in time each proves to be as
missing as the missing link.

13. Evolution doesn't even have enough
credibility to qualify itself as a
scientific theory.

14. There isn't just mountains OF evidence
for intelligent design—the mountains
ARE evidence.

15. Jonah being swallowed by a whale is easy to
believe because it involves the Supernatural.
What's hard to believe is that anyone could
swallow the stupidity of evolution.

16. He who insists that evolution has evidence
proves himself to be ever-dense.

17. It is an intellectual embarrassment to know
that there are those of our species, who, in
an effort to accommodate the senselessness
of believing that nothing created everything,

redefine the word "nothing" to be something, and then proclaim themselves to be intelligent.

18. Evolution is an insult to primates.

19. Evolution: the belief that peaceful primates have a common ancestor with murderous, lying, thieving, adulterous, hate-filled, blaspheming human beings.

20. Evolution doesn't even have a bone of contention.

21. If evolution was put on trial, the case would be dismissed because of a lack of evidence.

22. Those who believe that there is no intelligent design are their best argument for their argument that there was no intelligent design.

23. The burden of proof lies with the believer in evolution.

24. The extraordinary claims of evolution require extraordinary evidence, of which there is none that doesn't require faith.

25. Evolution rests entirely on a foundation of faith in what the believer in evolution has been told.

26. Those who say that they were not intelligently designed, certainly seem as though they weren't.

27. He who believes in evolution stands on a mountainous graveyard of failed and changing theories.

28. Those who believe in evolution and the Bible call the Son of God a liar, because He said that God made us in His image and as male and female.

29. The millions who believe in the fallacy of evolution are a testimony to the gullibility of humanity.

30. Most believers in evolution don't even know the difference between adaptation and Darwinian evolution.

31. A-posing thumbs, the evolution believers defense on Judgment Day.

32. Every atom of Nature screams intelligent design.

33. The most intelligent cannot create an atom from nothing and thinks he's intelligent when he maintains that Nature isn't intelligently designed.

34. Evolution stands in the way of the science of discovery; summed up in Einstein's "I want to know how God created this world."

SLIGHTLY HUMOROUS:

1. Support your local undertaker. Smoke cigarettes.

2. Why is it that prosperity preachers always want you to plant your seed in the soil of their garden?

3. Riddle. Why is one third of Jerusalem a clue that the USA should back Israel?

4. Giving a piece of pizza to a skeptic can be worth a thousand persuasive words. Besides, it stops his mouth.

5. To compare Jesus of Nazareth to any of the great historical leaders is like comparing the noonday sun to anemic glowworms.

6. Prosperity preachers have made themselves popular by dropping the letter "L" into the name of GOD.

7. Comparing Jesus with the greatest of human leaders is like comparing the sun to a flashlight with no batteries.

8. Man has a God-shaped vacuum in his head.

9. God intelligently designed the human brain, but He left it up to us to use it.

10. The resurrection of Jesus Christ was the undertaker's pink slip.

11. He who believes that it is harder for a rich man to enter heaven than for a needle to go through the eye of a camel, doesn't know his Bible.

12. The cynic who first said, "There's no such thing as a free lunch" never read in the gospels about loaves and fishes.

13. An introvert church is like Christmas lights in the daytime.

ENCOURAGEMENT

14. We are ever in the presence of an all-seeing holy Creator—an uncomfortable thought

for the ungodly, but oh so comforting for the Christian.

15. Each of us live on borrowed time and God is the Lender.

16. The world's biggest loser is he who dies without the Savior.

17. The word "evil" turned backwards spells "live," and if we want to live, we must turn evil backwards through repentance.

18. The Resurrection will nail the lid on the coffin of death forever.

19. The world's combined riches are like massive debt compared to the wealth the poorest believer has in Christ.

20. The unique and unseen beauty of the snowflake is a picture of the individual believer in Christ.

21. Never be discouraged by the humiliation of mockery. Be honored to bear the reproach of Christ and His cross.

22. Gold is of no value to a child, and the gospel is of no value to those who are childish in thinking.

23. God's great faithfulness remembered those in the Ark, and He remembers us in Christ because His mercies are new every morning.

24. Jesus took the period off the end of our death sentence.

25. Politics shakes the branches. The gospel takes an axe to the root of the tree.

26. Yesterday is a memory, tomorrow is a dream, and only today is a reality...so make it count for eternity.

27. Make Heaven the object of your rejoicing and treat everything else as mere icing on the cake.

28. Sit on wells and look up sycamore trees. You never know where you will find a divine encounter.

29. God uses people without talent.

30. The first step towards conversion is humility.

31. Conscience is given by God, shaped by society, and ignored by the rebellious.

32. As "vessels of honor" we must pour ourselves out for this dying world.

33. Christianity is the only religion that is continually singing in worship, because it has something to sing about.

34. The big hand on the clock of time will in time sweep all of us into eternity.

35. To trust in religion rather than in the Savior is to put trust in a shredded parachute.

36. The deepest valley can be a mountaintop experience, if we trust God in it and grow because of it.

37. If someone wrongs us, we shouldn't feel "hurt" and or a sense of resentment. We should see it solely as a divine test

of the depth of our love.

38. Tight-lipped with gossip, loose-lipped with the gospel.

39. Misconceptions never give birth to truth.

40. We don't mean to sound "superior" to other religions, but Christianity is the only religion that guarantees everlasting life. The parachute that works is by default the best.

41. In Christ, God has taken the sting out of death. In the light of eternity, nothing else really matters.

42. Reverse the word "evil" and you get to "live." Turn from evil and you get to live in Christ.

43. Don't listen to the devil even if he promises you the world. This world is temporal. God's Kingdom is eternal.

44. Don't over-listen to the joy-killing negative news of this hopeless world.

45. This world may have forsaken God, but it is not yet a God-forsaken world.

46. Each tombstone stands as a sobering reminder that "It's appointed to man once to die, and after this the Judgment."

47. Pity the poor billionaire who doesn't possess the riches of Jesus Christ.

48. The hands' ten digits remind us that the Ten Commandments will condemn those who violate its perfect precepts.

49. Mercy is a cracked damn that is holding

back His wrath against sin.

50. A surrendered will always seeks God's smile above our own.

51. What a wonderful God we serve, and what a wonder that we get to serve Him.

52. It would have been easier to contain a thousand suns than for death to hold the Savior.

53. The tiny beat of the resurrected heart of the Son of God had implications that resounded throughout the universe.

FAITH

1. Faith in God is the small rudder that can turn this sinful world around. A grain of faith can move mountains of sin.

2. Faith in God produces a confident courage, and deep consolation that keeps His promises.

3. Faith is the divine oxygen hose.

4. If you want God to use you in big things, be a servant of God in small things.

5. I appreciate what I am in Christ because I know what I am without Him.

6. When we hear of someone dying—no matter how young or old, how rich, or how famous, our hearts should ache with one sobering question—did they know the Lord?

7. To "believe" in God doesn't just mean to believe in His existence. That's axiomatic.

It means to trust in Him as you would a banker, a pilot, or a close friend.

8. Trusting in God can move us from cowardice to courageous, in a moment of time.

9. Let every sparrow always remind you of the provision of God.

10. Those who live without faith in Jesus Christ will eventually end up bitter, afraid, and disappointed.

LOVE

1. In the Gospel we have the summer of God's love, the autumn of His grace, the winter of His wrath, and the spring of His mercy.

2. God is like the sun, in that He gives light and life to those on whom He shines; but the warmth of His love is hidden from those who remain under the dark cloud of sin.

3. God's mercy is an ever-replenishing infinite ocean of pure love.

4. We know little of love until we have seen the blood of the cross.

5. Meditate much on the cross, for that is where you see the love of God.

6. Justice made Hell my destiny, but mercy made Heaven my home.

7. Love is the inoculation for the disease of the fear of man.

8. Dig into the bunker of the love of God, and

stay low until this battle is over.

9. If humanity loved God, we would have no need of police and prisons, judges and juries, locks and lawyers, guns and guards.

10. The cross makes the believer forever grateful and forever-minded.

11. No matter how dark the clouds, the sun still shines, and no matter how dark the day, we have the light of God's love.

12. The love of God, the Son of God.

13. There has never been an expression of love as was seen when God in human form was impaled on a cross.

14. See an Apostle of love in every Christ-hating Saul of Tarsus.

SIN AND JUDGMENT

1. No party, no joy, no pleasure, no mercy, no hope in Hell.

2. The Old Testament is summed up in one sentence: God promised to destroy death. The New Testament tells us how He did it.

3. The Christian doesn't do good works to earn his way to Heaven, but out of gratitude for the free gift of eternal life.

4. The most convinced of skeptics cannot disagree with the Bible when it says that sin is pleasurable.

5. It is a fateful but blessed blow to the human ego to believe the proverb "He who trusts

his own heart, is a fool."

6. Refuse the vaccine of the gospel, and perish by the disease of sin.

7. The biggest loser is he who dies in his sins.

8. Faith in God isn't an intellectual belief that He exists. It's an implicate trust in His impeccable integrity.

9. Death is the final storm that will convince those who ignore the teachings of Jesus, that they have built their house on sand.

10. He who has seen the love of God expressed in the cross, is no stranger to tears of gratitude.

11. The folly of the unbiblical practice of getting "decisions for Jesus" from kids is seen when they hit the teenage years and the opposite sex becomes of more interest than Noah and his ark.

12. Sinful man is a fist-shaking anemic flea under the foot of his elephantine Creator's wrath.

13. The human iris, in time, adjusts itself to darkness. So does the human heart to evil.

14. Preachers who talk about everything but the reality of Hell, are likeable betrayers of the gospel.

15. The world's thoughtless maxims, such as "He had his demons" "As sure as hell" and "I'll be damned," make me shudder to the core.

16. If I can't hate sin for what it is, I must hate

it for what it does.

17. Sin is the flame. Man is the moth.

18. The best of Christians know that they are the worst of sinners.

19. Sin is the opiate of the masses.

20. Those who find themselves guilty on Judgment Day will wish that we had convinced them of the truth of Scripture.

21. A world deceived by the pleasures of sin, enslaved to death and on its way to Hell, is a tragedy beyond words.

22. Sin is the deadly poison. The gospel is its only anecdote.

23. Beware of the subtle deceit of conceit. It is an obesity that delights itself in secret gratification.

24. This life, will all its joys and pleasures, is futile without God. It just takes some longer than others to realize it.

25. A calloused conscience will end up dead to the truth.

26. Sin deceives, degrades, and damns.

27. The Prodigal son came to his senses the moment he realized that his appetites were unclean. So is the way of the penitent sinner.

28. The dark shadow of God's wrath is instantly dissipated in the light of the cross.

29. The cross is a beacon of God's mercy amidst the dark storm of His terrible wrath.

30. The blood of Christ is the delete button for

sin and death.

31. This sinful world is spinning on an icy downhill road of moral relativity, and doesn't even know it.

32. The human conscience means that he who sins, sins in the light.

33. The world's ignores the pure waters of Christianity and drinks salt water of sins pleasure.

PRAYER

1. Much of our praying could be condensed into a simple, "Lord, make me more like Jesus."

2. Tears in our prayers produce passion in our preaching.

3. "God help us!" is the only necessary prayer of the contemporary Church.

4. May our praying and preaching be with hearts of compassion and tears of empathy.

5. It is prayer in the closet that puts a fire in the pulpit.

6. We can see further, hear better, and think clearer, when we are on our knees.

7. Lord make me hunger after truth, pray without ceasing, and plead with the lost like there is no tomorrow.

8. Tribulation drives us to the safety of our knees.

Evangelism

1. God forbid that we should be more concerned about personal persecution than we are about sinners being damned forever.

2. Our job is simply to sow the seed of the gospel and leave the rest up to God.

3. I am both a coward and a hypocrite if I believe that the world is going to Hell, but fail to verbally warn them.

4. Evangelism is the heartbeat of the local church. Those who don't feel its beat are close to expiration.

5. There will be no satisfaction in saying "I told you so" to the unsaved.

6. In too many churches the life—blood of evangelism has been drained to deathly irrelevance. Passionate prayer *for* the lost will manifest itself in passionate preaching *to* the lost. Has your pastor love enough to warn the lost about the reality of Hell? Either way, he needs your prayers.

7. Our evangelistic zeal will be in direct proportion to the depth of our love.

8. Run at Goliath. The very act of doing something in faith will help you overcome your fears.

9. What part of "Go" doesn't the contemporary Church understand?

10. Share the gospel regularly and you will

experience the miraculous reality of
John 14:21.

11. The preaching of God's Law puts salt on
the tongue of a sin-loving world that has no
thirst for righteousness.

12. It is a sobering statistic of more than
150,000 people today will make plans for a
tomorrow that will never come.

13. We preach to you, not because we want
something *from* you, but something *for* you.

14. I wouldn't have an ounce of evangelistic zeal
if it wasn't for the reality of Hell.

15. Emergency vehicles demand access because
human lives are at stake. Evangelism
demands the same priority, for the
same reason.

16. If you are sharing your faith, be ready for
sugar-coated discouragement from those
who don't.

17. Evangelism is like diving into an unheated
swimming pool. It takes courage to take the
plunge, but the flesh quickly adjusts.

18. A church that is waiting for sinners to visit
their building is like the police waiting for
criminals to visit their station.

19. Be steadfast in your evangelism. Learn a
lesson from the tortoise and the hare.

20. Preach about God's love and the world will
give you a standing ovation. Mention sin
and they will hate you as they hated Jesus.

21. Be a weapon in the hands of God with the aim of loving dying humanity.

22. Practice until presenting of the gospel comes as easy to you as eating barbecued ribs come to a hungry redneck.

23. May God give us the gentleness of a dove and the boldness of a lion, to say what we know we should.

24. The friendly preacher who fails to warn of the reality of Hell, betrays the Son of God with a kiss.

25. He is a cold-hearted coward who stands in a pulpit and doesn't sound the alarm about the reality of Hell.

26. Look deep into the eyes of a hellhound world and you will find it difficult to pass them by.

27. There is no more hated doctrine than that of eternal judgment. Those who fail to warn this sinful world of this biblical truth are cold-hearted and cowardly-sleeping sentries, Judas Iscariots, who betray the cause of the gospel for the applause of the world.

28. Gratitude is the high octane of zeal for the lost.

29. Keep your feet on the rock of God's promises, your eyes on Jesus, and your hands stretched out to this dying world.

30. The compass always faces north. The Christian always points to Jesus. Anything

else, is to head in the wrong direction.

31. Lord, help me to be a kind but uncompromising vessel of truth.

32. "Hate speech" is to believe that Hell exists and to speak about anything but its existence.

33. Change the heart with the gospel and you will change the mind. Change minds and you can change the world.

34. Humanity is a four-day-dead Lazarus whose only hope is in the life-giving words of Jesus Christ

35. Light is proof that there are unseen batteries in the flashlight. So let your light shine before men.

36. It is frustration indeed to be living in a Hell-bound world that won't listen.

37. Millions sit in the dark shadow of death not knowing the light and warmth of God's love.

38. There is nothing good about Good Friday, until we fall at the foot of that bloody cross and whisper, "For me He dies."

39. The cross of Jesus Christ is a beam of bright light in the darkness of death, saying "This is the way."

40. Life begins at the foot of the cross.

41. It will take eternity to express our gratitude for what God did for us in the cross of Jesus Christ.

42. Every day is Good Friday, for those who

have seen the cross.

43. Easter Sunday. The day we remember that death died.

44. Worship picks up where words leave off, when it comes to our adoration for the Giver of life and the Conqueror of death.

45. Eloquence falls short in expressing the power and majesty of God. It simply comes back to Andrew's words to Nathaniel: "Come and see."

46. As the resurrected Savior whispered the name of Mary, so He whispered our name as we passed from death to life at the moment of conversion.

47. I am constantly driven to my knees with an overwhelming frustration for a lack of words to communicate the treasure we have in Christ.

Extra Words of Comfort

Firestorm

Who would have believed that a storm or a fire could be good for a forest; but they are. The trauma of a storm shakes the trees causing them to send their roots deeper into the soil. A fast-moving fire in a pine forest burns up unwanted dead vegetation as well as opening tightly sealed cones, so that the seeds may be released and take root. So, life's normally frightening storms cause the Christian to grow in maturity, sending him closer to God and deep into His Word. The fiery trials help us to overcome our fears and open our lips to release the precious life-giving seed of the gospel into a dying world.

Scientific Breakthrough

Scientists recently called a news conference and announced a huge scientific breakthrough. They have designed a machine that turns grass-cuttings into milk. A spokesperson said the brilliantly made machine grinds the grass through rows of metal "teeth," and then sends it to a total of four different compartmental containers that contain chemicals that turn the green liquid substance into white milk. He also said that the machine could be broken down at any time and used for clothing and food. He then smiled and said the obvious. The announcement was a joke, because scientists didn't have a clue how to make grass from nothing that would turn into milk, then cream, cheese, butter, yoghurt and ice cream, let alone a machine that could do what the cow does as well as provide leather and meat for human consumption.

Some non-thinkers believe that the cow had no Designer. They believe that it was merely the result of nothing causing rocks that came from nowhere to explode for no reason. Then the scientifically impossible happened—non-life produced life. Sure.

HAWK-EYE

When a hawk is around, other birds hide for fear of their lives leaving an eerie silence in the trees. They instinctively know their enemy. It seems that a bird brain works better than a human brain, because most human beings don't see death as their "enemy." They think that it's just part of life. But around death, the ungodly have an eerie silence. They are defeated by it. They roll over and die. The Bible speaks of death as an enemy, saying that Jesus Christ has "abolished death and brought life and immortality to light through the gospel." Of course, many don't believe that, and that's their problem. They refuse to trust the Word of God, and yet trust is the basis for any relationship, both horizontal and vertical.

HOW TO GET LIGHT

After I commented "God knows those that love Him," an atheist replied: "Thanks, Ray, that's a relief, because sometimes it sure seems complicated."

The whole issue is going to seem a mess until each of us experience genuine conversion. When the Apostle Paul wrote to the Christians at Ephesus, he said, "This I say, therefore, and testify in the Lord, that you should no longer walk as the rest of the Gentiles walk, in the futility of their mind, having their understanding darkened, being alienated from the life of God, because of the ignorance that is in them, because of the blindness of their heart; who, being past feeling, have given themselves over to lewdness, to work all uncleanness with greediness" (Ephesians 4:17–18). Until we come to Christ our understanding is darkened, we are ignorant, blind, and given to the pleasures of sin, held captive to unlawful passions. With this thought in mind, read this verse from John 8:31–32 through three or four times: "Then said Jesus to those Jews which believed on him, If you continue in my word, then are you my disciples indeed; And you shall know the truth, and the truth shall make you free."

FOOL'S PARADISE

A professing Christian who denies the reality of Hell is like an airline worker who tells passengers they don't need a parachute, because gravity doesn't exist. He gives them a friendly pat on the back as each one jumps to their death. Charles Spurgeon, the Prince of Preachers, put it this way: "Ho, ho, sir surgeon, you are too delicate to tell the man that he is ill! You hope to heal the sick without their knowing it. You therefore flatter them; and what happens? They laugh at you; they dance upon their own graves. At last they die! Your delicacy is cruelty; your flatteries are poisons; you are a murderer. Shall we keep men in a fool's paradise? Shall we lull them into soft slumbers from which they will awake in Hell? Are we to become helpers of their damnation by our smooth speeches? In the name of God we will not."

UNLESS YOU REPENT

"Maybe Ray could tell me where his God was when the earthquake hit Christchurch, New Zealand...or did those people deserve to die?"

You have asked a very similar question to that which was asked of Jesus 2,000 years ago. Certain people came to Him and spoke of a large tower that fell down and tragically took the lives of 18 men. The inference was the same as yours. Did these people do something wrong? Jesus said, "Or those eighteen on whom the tower in Siloam fell and killed them, do you think that they were worse sinners than all other men who dwelt in Jerusalem? I tell you, no;

but unless you repent you will all likewise perish" (Luke 13:4–8).

There is a tendency in many religions to think that when there are mass deaths through a natural disaster (earthquake, tsunami etc.,) that God punished those who died. However, Jesus didn't directly address that question. He rather addressed those who were living about their own wickedness. The dead were dead and gone, but those who were still alive could be forgiven their sins, and that was the immediate issue.

You and I have greatly sinned against God and if He allowed His Law to fall upon us in its wrath, it would certainly crush and immediately damn each of us to Hell. But God is rich in mercy and offers us Heaven, if we repent and trust alone in the Savior.

ZEDEKIAH'S LAST SIGHT

The Bible is one of the most violent books ever written. It's filled with murder, rape, genocide, incest, babies being ripped from wombs, decapitations, and much more material for nightmares. It's 66 books in one, and is the history of the Hebrew nation. Its bloody message stands out in all its starkness—that Mankind is evil, and this evil nature is seen in what he does to his fellow man. It reads like the nightly news.

One gory story is the end of the reign of King

Zedekiah. God continually warned him (through His prophet) that he would be taken captive by the cruel Babylonians. In His great kindness, God also told him how to avoid coming to a bloody end. But Zedekiah refused to believe Jeremiah's warnings, and in time found himself at the mercy of the Babylonian king, who slaughtered Zedekiah's sons in front of his eyes, and then gauged the king's eyes out so that the last thing Zedekiah saw was the unspeakable horror of seeing his precious sons having their throats cut.

Tell me, do you think that Zedekiah regretted not believing God's warning, and His kind offer of mercy? "Regret" wouldn't be the applicable word for his emotions. Think about what he witnessed. Be the king for a moment. Feel his emotions. Then think what it would feel like to have someone take their thumbs, gouge out your precious eyes, and leave you in agonizing blackness.

No, "regret" is too weak a word. It could only be "remorse." It's the strongest word we have for such a horror, and remorse will be the eternal emotion of those who refuse the merciful warning of coming divine justice, and the offer of forgiveness in Jesus Christ. If they die in their sins they will be damned by a morally perfect and utterly holy God, who will see to it that perfect justice is done. We must let such sobering thoughts spur us on to reach the lost. If you are not born again and trusting alone in Jesus, please, oh please, check out www.needGod.com

OUTSIDE SOURCE

Have you ever wondered what it's like to be blind, to be starving, have chronic asthma, or a terminal disease? Are you thankful that you can see and breathe, that you have enough food, and that you are alive? How would you feel if you gave a person some very valuable gifts, and they simply snatched them from your hand and walked off? I did that for 22 years of my non-Christian life. To my absolute shame, I never even thought to thank God for the miracle of sight, for my food, for the ability to breathe, or for the wonderful gift of life. Not for one moment. Like the stench of bad breath and reeking body odor, the wickedness of ingratitude isn't self-detectible. That revelation needs to come from an outside Source.

ATHEIST QUIZ

See if you can guess the identity of these two famous atheists. The first was a minister of a large church when he converted to atheism, and the second atheist was a strong believer in evolution who became instantly famous around the globe, back in 1994:

1. "Our people, I would say, are ninety percent atheist...I felt somewhat hypocritical for

the last years as I became an atheist...My bishop knows that I'm an atheist...He must have spent twenty thousand dollars traveling around, hoping to get my denomination to remove me, because I was so atheistic."

2. "If a person doesn't think there is a God to be accountable to, then what's the point of trying to modify your behavior to keep it within acceptable ranges? That's how I thought anyway. I always believed the theory of evolution as truth that we all just came from the slime. When we died, you know, that was it, there is nothing ..."

Answers: 1. The first atheist was the Rev. Jim Jones of Jonestown and Peoples Temple. He led 909 men, women, and children in mass suicide in 1978 (quotes from: Transcript of Recovered FBI tape Q 622). 2. The second atheist and evolution believer was, Jeffrey Dahmer, who murdered seventeen men and boys, dismembering them, storing their parts and indulging in cannibalism and necrophilia. Quote taken from an interview with Stone Phillips, *Dateline NBC* (29 November 1994)

PROVING GOD

Skeptics mock the thought that the existence of God can be proved scientifically. But the word "science" simply means "knowledge." Creation (Nature) gives us knowledge that there's a Creator (a Maker). It is scientifically impossible for Nature to have made itself. To say that it did, is to say that it was pre-existent to be able to make itself, before it made itself, which is ludicrous. So each of us has an intuitive knowledge that God exists, and because of our conscience ("con" is "with" and "science" is "knowledge") we are "with knowledge" that we are morally responsible to Him. The building gives us knowledge there was a builder. The painting gives us knowledge there was a painter.

Of course, buildings and paintings are inorganic (non-living) and so are great mountains, vast oceans, and the massive clouds—"The heavens declare His glory." However, the existence of living forms (including ourselves) gives us even more light into the genius of God's creative hand—that we are "fearfully and wonderfully made," so that we are without excuse. No one needs faith to know that God exists. All we need are eyes that can see and a brain that works. However, if we want to approach Him, then we must have trust, for without an implicit trust it is impossible to please Him (see Hebrews 11:6).

LOST GLASSES

When my wife lost her reading glasses we turned the house upside down looking for them, and finally gave up. We had purchased something at a store the day before they disappeared, so without telling

Sue, I went there the next day and sure enough, they had them. I was so excited I could hardly wait to get back home and give them to my beloved wife. They were just a pair of glasses, but having been lost and now found made them very special.

The incident reminded me of a quick succession of three biblical stories in a row about lost things. One was about a woman who lost a gold coin. She too turned her house upside down until she found it, and it was such a big deal to her she called her friends over to celebrate. Then there's the story Jesus told of a shepherd who lost one of his sheep. He left his whole flock of 99 to search for it, and when he found it he came back rejoicing, carrying it on his shoulders—it was such a big deal. Then He told the famous story of the Prodigal Son who spent his money on prostitutes, and ended up desiring to eat pig food. He came to his senses and returned to his beloved father who welcomed him with open arms. He was lost, now he was found; dead and he had come alive.

Each of those stories is a picture of those of you who don't know the Lord. You may not think of yourself as "lost," but you are when you don't know where you came from, what you are doing here, or where you are going when you die. You are lost and don't even know it, and you are hopelessly condemned to death, and after that you will face what the Bible calls fearsome judgment. Yet despite your contempt for your Creator, you are of great value to Him. He values you enough to make provision for the forgiveness of your sins. You are lost, but can be found. Dead, but can be made alive. Please, soften your hard heart and listen to the gospel again, for the first time: www.needGod.com

SHUTTING OFF THE MAIN

An atheist is like a man who shuts off the main before he walks into an electrical store, and mocks the fact that the appliances don't work. Remove the supernatural from the Bible and nothing makes sense, because you have removed the power of God. Leave Him in the equation and animals fit comfortably onto the ark, the Red Sea opens no problem, the 5,000 get well fed, and water gets walked upon.

MAKING WATER

Imagine that you have a Petri dish in front of you. Here now is a biological experiment for you to conduct. Make one small drop of water. Begin with nothing in the dish, and don't use any existing materials. You will first need to produce hydrogen atoms from nothing, and then oxygen atoms using the same process. Then combine one oxygen atom for every two hydrogen atoms. This could take you some time as there are an estimated 1.67 sextillion molecules of H_2O in a drop of water.

Step two—You will need to make an amazingly complex phenomenon called "surface tension." This gives the water the ability to resist external forces. In other words it will allow certain insects to land on the surface without sinking. The liquid needs to be drinkable, to be able to evaporate, freeze, boil, cook, cleanse, as well as be able to be used for swimming, surfing, waterskiing, ice skating, ice hockey, snow skiing and snowboarding. Also, make it so that it will quench human thirst.

Just this manufacturing of one drop will make you instantly rich and famous, because it will mean an end to droughts, and the billions of acres of dry soils around the world will become fertile and therefore food-producing. It will mean an end to starvation.

Here's a quick intelligence test for you to do before you start the experiment. Do you believe that water is intelligently designed? If you say that no intelligence was involved in its construction (and yet you haven't a clue how to begin to make water yourself), where does that leave you on the intelligence scale?

CARRYING A GUN

"Jesus would never have carried a gun. A Christian with a gun is a fake Christian."

I don't carry a gun, but I wouldn't condemn someone who wanted to protect his family from an armed intruder. Neither should you. There are millions of fake Christians who don't carry guns. Love is the criteria, not whether or not someone carries a gun. One other thing. If you were in a public place and some nut was shooting children, would you be pleased to see a Christian take him out? Or would you be happy to let him continue killing kids? I'm sure you would want the murderer to be stopped. Jesus is not the person you make Him out to be. The Bible says that He's coming in flaming fire to bring vengeance on the disobedient. He doesn't need a gun to deal with evil.

THE BEATLES

"Lennon and McCartney met in the church because it was a convenient and quiet place to meet. Period. Lennon was an avowed atheist. Just listen to the lyrics of the brilliant 'Imagine'. He specifically weaves the sentence 'and no religion too' into this musical masterpiece. George was so Christian that he was Hindu."

You sure need to read, *The Beatles, God, and the Bible*. In 1964/65 Paul McCartney, when asked if they believed in God, said that none of them did. But as each of The Beatles began to mature in their thinking, each one became spiritual. Lennon said that "Imagine" was a prayer (see his Playboy Interview—Google it). His said "imagine" was a prayer that people stop fighting over who had the right God, over countries, over possessions, etc. He said he wasn't saying that there's no Heaven. Just the opposite. If I said to you, "Imagine there's no New York," I'm saying let's imagine (pretend) New York doesn't exist. Imagining it doesn't exist is an admittance that it does. George said his whole life was a search for God.

GET YOUR BRAIN WORKING

Did you know that an estimated six million people in the United States have an unruptured brain aneurysm—that's one in every 50 people? If a blood vessel suddenly explodes in your brain, you won't even be able to think "God help me!" So get your brain into action today (while it is working), and make peace with the God you have so greatly offended. See www.needGod.com if you are interested in eternal life.

HOW TO WITNESS TO HOMOSEXUALS

Homosexuality is a hot issue. Open your mouth against it nowadays, no matter how casually or even lovingly, and you will almost certainly be accused of using "hate speech." There is, however, a way around this for the Christian.

When I meet a homosexual, I never talk about his sexual orientation. This is because I care about him and want to share the gospel, and I don't want him to be offended before I do that. So I witness to him the way I witness to any heterosexual. I ask if he thinks he's a good person. When he predictably says that he is, I take him through the Ten Commandments—has he lied, stolen, and blasphemed God's name? When I ask about lust (see Matthew 5:27–28), I don't mention gender. After seeing his transgressions in the light of God's Law he will understand his guilt—and that he's headed for Hell and desperately in need of the Savior.

Before he saw his sin, he was proud and self-righteous, but now he's humble of heart. That means he is able to be reasoned with, without being defensive. So I tell him that to be saved he must repent of all sin and trust alone in Jesus. I then show him what "sin" is, by referring to 1 Corinthians 6:9–10 (which lists those who will not enter the Kingdom of Heaven): "Do not be deceived. Neither fornicators, nor idolaters, nor adulterers, nor homosexuals, nor sodomites, nor thieves, nor covetous, nor drunkards, nor revilers, nor extortioners will inherit the kingdom of God." I gently tell him that if he has a problem with the list, he should take it up with God, because it's His list.

Is it biblical to use the moral Law (the Ten Commandments) when speaking with homosexuals? It certainly is: "But we know that the law is good if one uses it lawfully, knowing this: that the law is not made for a righteous person, but for…fornicators, for sodomites, for kidnappers, for liars, for perjurers, and if there is any other thing that is contrary to sound doctrine" (1Timothy 1:8–10).

For further teaching on biblical evangelism please freely listen to "Hell's Best Kept Secret" on www.livingwaters.com

FEAR TACTICS

When I recently said that one in 50 people have an aneurism that's waiting to burst, a number of atheists accused me of using fear tactics to manipulate weak people. One posted two or three times protesting. When asked by a Christian if she was afraid of dying, she was quick to respond: "I fear the potential of pain during the process of death as is only natural but death itself is not scary. I won't be there to care about it…I cannot be afraid of nothing." But I have it from a trustworthy Source that she was lying. Strong words, but true. She was lying through her terrified teeth. The Bible says that all of humanity are "all of their lifetime" haunted by the fear of death (see Hebrews 2:14–15). Some drown their terror in alcohol or drugs. Some busy themselves so that they don't think about it, and the proud play the bravado card.

Most people think that fear is bad, but, if you will let it, fear can be your friend. It's fear that makes you buckle up your seat belt (fear of pain or the police). Fear makes a sky-diver put on a parachute. It keeps us from the danger of a thousand foot cliff-edge. Fear can be self-preserving, if you will let it. So listen to its alarming voice, let it send you to the only One that can save you from death and release you from "fear that has torment." See www. needGod.com for details.

BELIEF IN FOSSILS

An atheist recently wrote "When are you coming to see the fossils with me, Ray?" It seems that he thought that I didn't believe in fossils. How could I not? There are millions of fossils in museums all over the world. I have even seen thousands of fossils in the "Evolution" museum in Paris. I took a camera crew there a few years ago to look for the evidence for evolution, but they didn't even have an evolution display. All they had was a stuffed monkey in a back area, with "Lucy" written on it. I did the same thing with the Smithsonian in Washington DC. All they had was a family of hairy manikins, squatting around a fire. Every other display was simply examples of God's creation.

Of course I believe in fossils, but I don't believe in the unobservable bogus science called "evolution," of which there is no empirical evidence. Anything that is said to be evidence always necessitates faith. I don't believe because I'm a skeptic when it comes to evolution.

HEAVEN'S EXISTENCE

"When Christians get to their mythological Heaven, what will they do? Worship their God for billions and billions of years?"

I will do my best to try and explain the unexplainable. Let's imagine that I am there just before the six days of creation, and God says to me, "Try and imagine what I'm about to do?" I would have a problem, because I have nothing upon which to base my imaginations. I couldn't imagine that He was about to create 1.4 million different kinds of animals, birds, fish and insects. I wouldn't ponder the tall patch-worked yellow and black six-foot-necked giraffe, the massive floppy-eared elephant, the striped zebra, cute kittens, adorable dogs, roaring lions, growling tigers, and a mass of other amazing animals, all with male and female, and with the ability to bring forth after their own kind.

I couldn't think of massive snow-capped mountains, deep blue seas teeming with colorful fish of all sorts of shapes and sizes. Neither could I imagine, skiing, surfing, fishing, tasty food, the pleasures of the marital bed, and a thousand and one other delicacies of life.

Heaven isn't what the world imagines it to be. Those who enter won't be sitting on a cloud playing a rusty harp for eternity. God's kingdom is coming to this earth and His will, will be done on earth as it is in Heaven. Heaven is coming to this earth. No more earthquakes, tornadoes, hurricanes, disease, pain and death. The Bible says that this everlasting kingdom is beyond the human imagination. So think of the greatest most pleasurable thing on earth, and then whisper to yourself that is nothing more than the dregs of the bottom of a filthy trash bin, compared to what God has in store for those who love Him.

SUFFERING AND DEATH

I remember as a child looking into the back of a medical book and being horrified at seeing, not hundreds, but thousands of diseases each of us can get. As I grew in understanding, I found that I was part of the ultimate statistic—ten out of ten die. Everywhere I looked, there was disease, suffering and death. It was a though all humanity were willingly standing in a line, waiting to fall off a thousand foot cliff, and I wanted to know how I could get out of line.

There were a few explanations as to why death existed. 1. Evolution was responsible for all the beauty of Nature, but had somehow messed up with all the suffering and death. 2. There was no God, and all of Nature happened by chance. 3. God existed, but He was cold and impersonal—a tyrant who created all this pain.

However, the answer was none of the above, and it came from an unexpected source. When I was confronted with the Ten Commandments back on April 24th, 1972, I suddenly saw that I was very sinful in my Creator's eyes, and understood for the first time in my life that God so loved me that He provided a Savior to save me from Hell.

I repented, put my trust in Jesus, came to know the Lord, and was instantly a brand new person. It was more than a change of mind or lifestyle... much more. It was the miracle of the new birth of John chapter 3, and in that miracle came the answer to the mystery.

We live in a "fallen creation," under the wrath of a morally perfect God. Every disease, all the suffering and death is the result of our rebellion against our Creator. The Bible says that until we make peace with God, we are in darkness, so please, let today be the day that you come into the light. See www. needGod.com for details.

MY FATHER

My father used to hit me. He would daily leave my mother to raise us kids, and I once saw him kill a helpless animal with his bare hands. With that information you could understandably come to the conclusion that my father was a tyrant. But listen to some missing information. If I ever lied or stole, my dad cared enough to correct me on the seat of my learning, and for that I greatly respected him and stayed on the straight and narrow. The reason he left my mom each day was to work hard as a carpenter and provide food for our table. And that animal he killed... It was a large bird that had been struck by a car and had been left to die on the side of the road. He put the poor animal out of its misery, and it grieved him to do so. With that knowledge you can now see that my dad wasn't a tyrant. He was a loving and kind father.

Richard Dawkins believes that God is more than just a tyrant. He said, "The God of the Old Testament is arguably the most unpleasant character in all fiction: jealous and proud of it; a petty, unjust, unforgiving control-freak; a vindictive, bloodthirsty ethnic cleanser; a misogynistic, homophobic, racist, infanticidal, genocidal, filicidal, pestilential, megalomaniacal, sadomasochistic, capriciously malevolent bully."

But there's some missing information he's not giving you that changes everything...for those who will listen.

This same morally perfect and holy Creator (whose seeming harsh judgments were always "righteous and true altogether") became a morally perfect human being. He did this to save us from the same just wrath that spilled upon the wicked nations of the Old Testament. Most of us know that Jesus of Nazareth gave His life as a sacrifice for the sin of the world. What they don't know is that we violated God's Law (the Ten Commandments) and justly deserve the wrath of the moral Law, but Jesus paid our fine in full. That means that God can legally dismiss our case. He can commute our death sentence and let us live forever, because our fine was paid by Another who then rose from the dead.

The same holy God who considers lust to be adultery and hatred to be murder, made provision for His great love and mercy to be extended towards those who repent and trust in the Savior. For the Christian, the cross of Jesus Christ shows that God isn't the wicked tyrant that foolish and ignorant men make Him out to be. It is the missing information that changes everything.

WHICH RELIGION?

"I come from Israel. I live in society with three different religions, Judaism, Christianity and Islam…when I talk with any member of any religion, he says he's convinced that HIS religion is the right one, and the other two are wrong (atheists know that ALL three are wrong, but it's not the point)." Rabì Francis Hume

All the great religions (except Christianity) have one thing in common. They believe that in order to gain everlasting life they have to do sacrificial "good works" such as fasting, praying, good deeds, facing a certain way to pray, repentance for sin, etc. However, there's a big problem with such sacrifices.

Jesus expounded the Ten Commandments to include lust, hatred, and anger without cause. He said that if we as much as look with lust, we commit adultery in our hearts (Matthew 5:27–28). As Judge of the earth, God requires moral perfection, and in His eyes we are all desperate criminals that have been condemned to death. So any good works we offer God as Judge aren't seen by Him as "good works," but are attempts to bribe Him to forgive our sins, and the Bible says that God will not be bribed: "The sacrifice of the wicked is an abomination to the Lord."

However, this same holy God is rich in mercy, and He in His great kindness made a way for us to be forgiven by providing His own sacrifice. This was the hidden meaning of Abraham offering his "only begotten son," as a sacrifice. The Old Testament is full of these veiled "types," pointing forward to when God would provide the perfect sacrificial Lamb.

When the innocent Lamb of God was sacrificed on the cross, He was doing what none of us could do for ourselves. He was offering a perfect sacrifice that would satisfy the wrath of a morally perfect

God against our sin. He was paying our fine so that we could walk out of the courtroom. The suffering death and resurrection of Jesus of Nazareth meant that God could legally dismiss our case. He could commute our death sentence and let us live, because our fine was paid by Another.

Again, eternal life cannot be gained by any amount of religious works because it is an attempt to bribe the Judge. It can only come by the unmerited favor of God, and the Bible says that He is rich in mercy to all that call upon His name. He freely offers everlasting life to humanity as a gift. This is the ultimate good news for Islam, Judaism, Catholicism, Mormonism and all other religious folks who are trying in vain to earn everlasting life by their own sacrificial works. They simply have to repent and trust alone in the Savior, and in doing so God will grant what is called "imputed righteousness." He will give them a right standing with Himself, and extend His gracious of hand of mercy. The Bible says "whosoever" calls upon the name of the Lord shall be saved. If you are at all interested in everlasting life, please check out www.needGod.com

CONCLUSION

I banned a very nice orthodox priest from my Facebook page recently. He was polite, kind, respectful, friendly, and it seemed that he was always talking about the importance of love and forgiveness. However, after one of my posts he asked, "Why do you bring fear into the gospel?" The question was a little strange, so I asked if he believed in the existence of a literal Hell. After some hedging he revealed that he believed that Hell was "the fire of God's love," and he linked me to an article that said that it was disgusting to go around warning people about Hell. Up until that point I had already banned 1,449 atheists for cussing, and when the friendly priest joined them, I was suddenly flooded with angry protesting atheists who loved him. I told them that they were very welcome on my page, but any professing Christian who betrayed the cause of the gospel would be banned.

There are many preachers in pulpits that are like the popular priest. One atheist spoke of one when he commented, "I went to church four days ago. I liked the preacher because he didn't yell and scream and tell me I was going to Hell. He smiled the whole time he talked. Why can't more of them be like that?" I told him that it seemed that his smiley preacher (like the friendly priest), either didn't believe the words of Jesus, or he didn't care that people who die in their sins would end up in Hell.

These are, however, difficult times for the average preacher. If we warn of Hell or speak of the Bible's stance on homosexuality, we are quickly accused of hate speech. But there are ways that you and I can talk about the reality of Hell and reach homosexuals with the gospel, and have it make sense.

One reason preachers avoid speaking of Hell isn't because they don't believe in it. It's because they misunderstand the purpose of the moral Law (the Ten Commandments). God's Law shows us that the One we must face on Judgment Day is morally perfect, and that He considers lust to be adultery (see Matthew 5:27–28) and hatred to be murder (see 1 John 3:15). It is because of this perfect righteousness that He abhors evil and warns that a day of ultimate and perfect justice is coming. Any human judge who is good must see that justice is done, and God's goodness will see to it that ultimate justice will be satisfied. Murderers, rapists, thieves, liars, fornicators, adulterers, etc., will get what is due to them.

When preachers don't use the Law to show God's absolute righteousness, and instead talk of His love and kindess, adding "But He will send you to Hell if you don't trust in Jesus" makes no sense. It paints God as a vengeful tyrant. So any such talk is avoided.

However, when Paul reasoned with Felix, we are told that he spoke of sin (which is transgression of the Law—1 John 3:4), righteousness (which is of the Law) and temperance, and Felix "trembled."

In the light of his own exceeding sinfulness and the perfect righteousness of God, the self-indulgent governor understood that he was in big trouble. He trembled because Hell suddenly made sense. The Law makes Hell reasonable.

When I speak with a homosexual, I avoid talk about his sexual orientation. This is because I don't want him to be offended before I share the gospel. So I simply ask if he thinks he's a good person. When he predictably says that he is, I take him through the Ten Commandments (because scripture says that the moral Law was made for homosexuals—1 Timothy 1:8–10). Has he lied or stolen? Has he blasphemed God's name? And when I ask about looking with lust, I deliberately don't mention any gender.

Before seeing his sin, he was proud and self-righteous (thinking he was morally good), but now he's humble of heart. That means he is able to be reasoned with, without being defensive. So I tell him that to be saved from Hell he must repent of all sin and trust alone in Jesus. I then show him what "sin" is, by referring him to 1 Corinthians 6:9–10: "Do not be deceived. Neither fornicators, nor idolaters, nor adulterers, nor homosexuals, nor sodomites, nor thieves, nor covetous, nor drunkards, nor revilers, nor extortioners will inherit the kingdom of God." I then lovingly tell him that if he has a problem with the list, he should take it up with God, because it's His list, not mine.

I want to see adulterers, fornicators, thieves and others on that list avoid the terror of Hell, so why should I exclude homosexuals because I'm afraid of being accused of hatred. Love cannot do that.

Great preachers of past centuries understood the necessity of doing what Jesus did—using the Ten Commandments to bring the knowledge of sin (see Mark 10:17). A failure to do so has resulted in the Church being filled with false converts, and this has dissipated its ability to be salt and light in a dark and sinful world. It has relegated the Church to irrelevance in the eyes of the world (see Matthew 5:13). It's time to go back to biblical evangelism.

For further teaching on these principles please freely listen to "Hell's Best Kept Secret" on www.livingwaters.com